KIDS EXPLORE AMERICA'S AFRICAN AMERICAN HERITAGE

2nd edition

Westridge Young Writers Workshop

John Muir Publications
Santa Fe, New Mexico

Read this book and you will learn,
We, as all people, make the world turn.
Each person is different in his or her own way.
We want you to know that that's OK.
You can learn from these people as you will see.
This book is for you—given from me!

This book is dedicated to people of different cultures, with the hope
that they are proud of who they are.

John Muir Publications, P.O. Box 613, Santa Fe, NM 87504

Printed in the United States of America
Second edition. First printing October 1996

Library of Congress Cataloging-in-Publication Data
Kids explore America's African American heritage / Westridge Young
 Writers Workshop. — 2nd ed.
     p. cm.
   Summary: Presents writings by students in grades three to seven on topics of
African American culture, including recipes, games, history, art, sports, songs, and role models.
   ISBN 1-56261-271-9
   1. Afro-Americans—Juvenile literature. [1. Afro-Americans.
2. Children's writings.] I. Westridge Young Writers Workshop.
E185.K46   1993
973' .0496073—dc20   92-32275
                                                             CIP
                                                              AC

Editors Rob Crisell, Peggy Schaefer, Krista Lyons-Gould
Production Marie Vigil, Nikki Rooker
Graphics Manager Sarah Horowitz
Cover art Tony D'Agostino
Typesetting Marcie Pottern
Printer Publishers Press

Distributed to the book trade by
Publishers Group West
Emeryville, California

Photo credits: Photo on page 16 courtesy of Archive Photos/Consolidated News; photos on pages
                 5, 7, 8, 11, 13, 17, 19-20, 33, 37, 43-47, and 82 courtesy of the Schomberg Collection
                 of the New York Public Library; Angela Davis photo on page 20 by Philippe Halsman;
                 photo on page 23 courtesy of Archive Photos/Paul Slade; Bill Cosby photo on page 38
                 courtesy of Reuters/Jim Bourg/Archive Photos.

CONTENTS

ACKNOWLEDGMENTS / v

STUDENTS' PREFACE / vii

TEACHERS' PREFACE / ix

HISTORY / 1
Before America / 2
African Discoveries / 3
The Beginning of Slavery in America / 4
Emancipation / 7
Reconstruction / 9
The Road to Freedom / 10
Living through History:
  Carlotta Walls LaNier / 21
America Today / 24

FAMOUS FIRSTS AND HEROES / 29
Featured Biographies / 30
  Lucy Terry Prince / 30
  Benjamin Banneker / 31
  Bill Pickett / 32
  Leroy B. "Satchel" Paige / 32
  Thurgood Marshall / 33
  Jesse Owens / 34
  Jackie Robinson / 35
  Daniel "Chappie" James / 36
  Shirley Chisholm / 37
  Bill Cosby / 38
  Arthur Ashe / 38
  Mae Jemison / 40
Short Biographies / 41
  Estevanico Dorantez / 41
  Elizabeth Freeman / 41
  Olaudah Equiano / 42
  Norbert Rillieux / 42
  Elijah McCoy / 42
  Edmonia Lewis / 43
  Jan E. Matzeliger / 43
  Granville T. Woods / 43
  Daniel Hale Williams / 44
  Sarah B. "Madame C. J." Walker / 44

Charles Henry Turner / 45
Ida B. Wells / 45
William Christopher Handy / 45
Carter G. Woodson / 46
Bessie Coleman / 46
Bessie Smith / 46
Marian Anderson / 47
Ralph Bunche / 47
Gwendolyn Brooks / 48
Althea Gibson / 49
Wilma Rudolph / 49
More Famous Firsts and Heroes / 50

ART, MUSIC, AND DANCE / 53
Art / 54
  Early African Art / 54
  Adinkira Art / 54
  Drums / 57
  Rattles / 59
  African Art in the United States / 61
  Art Museums / 64
  Black Artists / 64
Music / 64
  Spirituals / 64
  Development of Modern African
    American Music / 66
  African American Performers / 68
Dance / 69
  African American Dancers / 72

FUN, FOOD, AND CELEBRATIONS / 74
Celebrations / 74
  Freedom Celebrations / 74
  Junkanoo / 75
  Kwanzaa / 76
  Honoring Black History / 77
  Honoring Martin Luther King Jr. / 77
  Honoring Malcolm X / 78
  Harambee / 78
  Traditional Gatherings of Friends
    and Family / 79
Foods / 79

Herbs / 80
   Fresh Mint Tea / 81
   Sassafras Tea / 81
Biscuits / 81
   Down-Home Biscuits / 82
Cornmeal / 82
   Cornbread / 83
   Corn Pone / 83
Black-Eyed Peas / 83
   Mom's Black-Eyed Peas /83
Greens / 84
   Home Greens / 85
Peanuts / 85
   Peanut Butter / 86
   Peanut Butter Banana
     Sandwich / 86
   Vegetable Peanut Butter
     Sandwich / 86
Bread Pudding / 86
Sweet Potato Pie / 87
Catfish / 87
   Fried Catfish Strips / 87
"Soul" Ice Cream / 88
Emancipation Proclamation
   Snackin' Cake / 88

**STORIES, LANGUAGE, AND
LITERATURE** / 90
Stories / 90
   "Brer Rabbit Gets Brer Fox's
     Dinner" / 91
   "Wiley and the Hairy Man" / 91
   "How the Turtle Got Marks on Its
     Shell" / 93
   "How the Sea Creatures Found Their
     New Home" / 94
   "Why Spiders Have No Hair" / 95
   "The People Could Fly" / 95
   "Follow the Drinking Gourd" / 96
   "The Talking Eggs" / 97
Language / 98
Literature / 99

REAL PEOPLE / 101
   Daryl Price / 102
   Dorothy Jenkins Fields / 103
   Leon Smith / 104
   Georgette Ajulufoh / 105
   Frank Hughes / 106
   Sylvia Kirk / 108
   Rodney Jones / 109
   Bill Potts / 110
   Carneice Brown White / 111
   Paul Stewart / 113
   Fatimah Linda Collier Jackson / 115
   Steve Floyd / 116

KIDS WHO MAKE A DIFFERENCE / 118
   Twyla Rivers / 118
   Roosevelt Johnson / 120
   Jessica Gray / 122
   Damon K. Jones-Singleton / 123
   Deshone Tabb / 125
   Kevin Parker / 126

**OUR VISION FOR A BETTER
TOMORROW** / 129

STUDENT AUTHORS / 131

TEACHER PARTICIPANTS / 132

MENTORS / 133

OTHER PARTICIPANTS / 133
   Columbine Elementary / 134
   St. Bernard's School / 134

CALENDAR / 135

RESOURCE GUIDE / 139

INDEX / 146

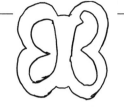

ACKNOWLEDGMENTS

We, the student authors, are especially appreciative of the people of African American heritage who shared their time and talents with us. We would also like to thank Westridge Elementary School, Columbine Elementary, St. Bernard's School, the Westridge PTA, Ron Horn, and all of our teachers and volunteers for their confidence in us as young writers and illustrators.

Special thanks goes to several businesses and organizations for their financial support. Student scholarships were donated by King Soopers of Denver, Colorado, and the Lakewood Civitan Club of Lakewood, Colorado. U.S. West and the First Bank of Lakewood, Colorado, have also contributed financial support to our program.

Many other people helped make this book a reality. They are acknowledged in a list of participants at the back of the book.

STUDENTS' PREFACE

As you read these pages, line by line,
Love and fun you're sure to find.
Whatever your color, it doesn't matter,
Look at the soul, not the sound of the chatter.
So listen to the words we tell,
They're loud and clear—just like a bell.
People are different, that's no lie.
Everyone's special like you and I.
Color, shape, size—they're no big deal,
It's what's inside you that is real.
Black or white, it's all the same,
So let's put an end to this silly game.
As you turn the pages of this book,
Turn around and take another look.
A perfect world the Earth would be,
A land of peace and harmony,
If people would just treat each other
As if they were a sister or a brother.

Beware! If you read this book, you will learn about parts of the African American heritage that you may not already know. This book is written by kids from a kid's point of view. We hope it's fun to read. We authors are in grades three through eight, and we worked very hard to share some of the information we learned.

We're excited because this book will help teach all people about the pride in African American heritage.

Kids Explore America's African American Heritage is not just for kids. Grown-ups can read and learn from it, too. We hope it will help make our world a fairer, more peaceful place in which to live.

TEACHERS' PREFACE

We accept the challenge of building a brighter future. We will not ignore the problems caused by racism in America. We pledge to continue to work for respect for all Americans.

The Kids Explore series is meant to be informative as well as to encourage a sense of pride in America's diverse heritages. The Westridge Young Writers Workshop is located at Westridge Elementary School in Jefferson County, a western suburb of Denver, Colorado. John Muir Publications of Santa Fe, New Mexico, enthusiastically brought its publishing assistance to our program. Together, we're working to increase children's respect and understanding of America's many cultures.

Kids Explore America's African American Heritage was written by students in grades three through eight. We,

the teachers and high school mentors, directed and assisted in writing and illustrating our exploration of African American culture. Students experienced many aspects of African American heritage, including history, heroes, celebrations, food, art, music, dance, folktales, language, and "real people." The writers explored these aspects of the culture, researched information, word processed, organized, wrote, proofread, and illustrated. After nine wonderful, hectic days, we celebrated everything we had learned together.

While our young authors enhanced their writing skills and enriched their knowledge of African American heritage, we earned graduate college credit through a course entitled "Integrating African American Studies into the School Curriculum."

Most of us are African American teachers, mentors, and students who live throughout the Denver metropolitan area. Most of us have lived in other parts of our country, and so we shared our diverse knowledge of our culture. We were an enthusiastic group, exploring ways to integrate African American culture into the curriculum and enriching our knowledge of publishing procedures and the writing process.

Although we all share a deep respect for the African American heritage, the most important thing we have

in common is a wish to increase the awareness of the diverse cultures that make up our country. We are a nation of risk-takers, innovators, and believers in a brighter tomorrow. We sincerely believe that if concerned individuals ignore the racism that is growing in our society, America will have even greater problems in the future. We have taken on the challenge to implement change in America's schools by writing a resource that can be used in homes and classrooms to teach understanding of our different heritages.

Remember to ask your bookstores, libraries, and schools about our book. Look in the back pages of this book for other titles in the Kids Explore series.

HISTORY

The history of blacks
Is often out of whack,
But our book has put it back.

We have struggled through time,
And we hope you keep in mind
That we are important to all mankind.

In this section, we talk about some of the important events that brought African Americans to where they are today. As you read, try to remember that sometime in your heritage—no matter what your race is—one of your ancestors may have been a slave. All races have been victims of slavery. For example, when the Romans conquered the Greeks, the Greek people became slaves to the Romans. If they didn't cooperate, they were killed. Lots of people celebrate Saint Patrick's Day, but they may not know that St. Patrick was once a slave of Irish tribes. African Americans are not the only people who have been slaves.

In this chapter, you will read that Africans had a rich heritage before they came to America. You will see that in America, which has a government based on a constitution that says everyone is created equal, African Americans didn't have freedom and weren't treated as equals. You will read how the slaves started to gain their freedom through the "underground railroad" and the Civil War. You will also read about the civil rights movement and the people who worked hard to give everyone equal rights by using such nonviolent methods as talking, petitions, sit-ins, and peaceful marches.

We hope you will learn not to judge people by their color but by their character. And we hope you will learn something new about African American history!

BEFORE AMERICA

The ancestors of African Americans made contributions to other cultures of the world that they have never gotten credit for. For example, lots of things found in Greek, European, and Asian cultures actually started in Africa. In fact, some scholars believe that humankind began in Africa. This is based on the fact that man-made tools more than 2 million years old were found in East Africa. For many years, people thought a skeleton found in Europe was the oldest evidence of humanity, then much older bones were discovered in Kenya. These bones are believed to be 4 million years old.

The land of Africa was—and still is—a rich land, not only because of the many resources (silver, gold, and diamonds), but also because the land has such a variety of landscapes. There are great deserts in the north, dense rain forests in the center, and great endless

plains in the south and along the coasts. But the most important resource was the people, who built nations and kingdoms long before the rest of the world did.

Egypt, on the northern coast of Africa, was not much more than a group of cities that had separate governments and worked independently. These city-states were made into the empire of Egypt around 3100 B.C. This was the first nation in Africa and one of the greatest in world history. It reached its height at about 1400 B.C. and produced many great rulers. One of these, Thutmoses III, ruled from about 1500 to 1450 B.C. This black leader controlled a kingdom 2,000 miles long and was known for his military power.

The kingdom of Kush, another nation located just south of the Egyptian empire, was founded about 1,000 years after Egypt united, lasting from 2000 B.C. to A.D. 350. Kush, which conquered Egypt in about 700 B.C., was the first African nation to specialize in iron mining and manufacturing. Around A.D. 300, an empire named Ghana began in the western part of Africa. This kingdom, the first major nation of West Africa, lasted about 1,000 years and was known for its wealth and trade. This nation was conquered by the Mandingo (Mandinka), a group of people it once ruled. The Mandingo people formed a nation called Mali, which means "where the Mansa (master or king) resides." The Mali kingdom lasted 200 years, stretching 1,500 miles eastward from the Atlantic Ocean. Mansa Musa, one of its leaders, who ruled from A.D. 1312 to 1337, established the Great University of Sankore in the city of Timbuktu. This university was one of the largest in the world. During this time, a group of West Africans (who became known as Moors)

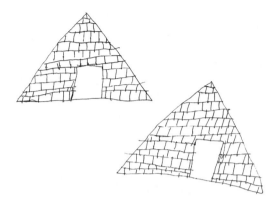

invaded, conquered, and ruled Spain for 700 years (A.D. 711 to 1400). The Moors, who were great shipbuilders and sailors, taught the Spanish people the skills of making maps and round globes, paving, and lighting streets.

We know that there were many more giant nations and rulers in Africa who also contributed much to civilization as we know it. We just wanted to tell you about a few of the nations that existed long before Europe was developed.

AFRICAN DISCOVERIES

Here are a few more examples of discoveries made by early Africans. An Egyptian contribution was the introduction of papyrus (paper). Another was the beginning of a belief in one God. The pharaoh (an Egyptian king) Akhenaton taught his people to believe in one God. Another wonderful African contribution was the university. In the beginning, it was called the Grand Lodge of Wa'at. This name was later changed by the Greeks, who called it Luxor. Imhotep, an African

man who lived in about 2800 B.C., is considered the father of medicine. Many sources state that the first doctor was Hippocrates, but Hippocrates was born 2,000 years after Imhotep. Some historians tell us that astronomy, map-making, and the solar calendar, as well as the basics of geometry, started in Africa. Geometry was used in the building of the pyramids as early as 2664 B.C., just as it has been used in constructing modern buildings such as the Eiffel Tower and the Washington Monument. The concepts of government and kings and queens originated in Africa as well.

We hope this information will help you understand why African Americans have such pride in their heritage. There are many books you can read to find out more about Africa.

THE BEGINNING OF SLAVERY IN AMERICA

Originally, not all the Africans in the colonies were slaves. Some were indentured servants. An indentured servant was a person who had to work for another person for no pay until his debt was paid in labor, usually a period of two to seven years. After indentured servants had completed their time, they would be given food, clothes, seeds, tools, and a little money to start their own life. White indentured servants sometimes escaped once they had arrived in America with their master. They could mix in with other whites

because their skin was fair, so they were hard to recapture. White settlers also tried to make Native Americans (Indians) their servants, but they felt that the Indians didn't make good slaves. They would often escape and go back to their tribes, or they would even kill themselves. White settlers started to bring in Africans to be their indentured servants and do their work for them. Unfortunately, people from Africa didn't remain indentured servants. Instead, something far worse happened—they became slaves.

Close your eyes and imagine you are sound asleep in your home. All of a sudden, a bunch of men burst into your room and kidnap you. You are placed in chains and sent on a long journey to a foreign country as a lifetime servant for a stranger.

This wasn't just a bad dream for the men, women, and children who became slaves in the American colonies. Conditions on the slave ships were horrible. Since money was so important, slave

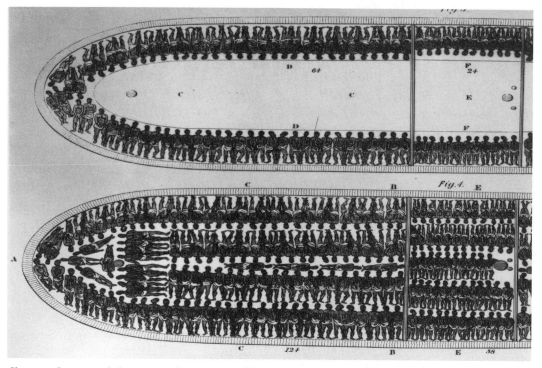

Slave traders crowded as many slaves as possible onto ships to increase profit.

traders almost always tried to bring as many people to the Americas as they could. Africans were packed in the cargo holds of ships. Many slaves even died at sea.

After slaves got off the ship from Africa, they were rounded up like cattle and taken to market for auction. Even if they came with their families, they would probably be split up. Life never got any better.

Many slaves were bought to work on plantations, which are big farms that raise corn, tobacco, beans, cotton, and cattle. In 1798, Eli Whitney invented an easier way of farming cotton, and that crop suddenly became a big money-maker. Whitney's invention was called

the cotton gin. It separated seeds by cranking the cotton through a small set of comblike teeth. Anyone with slaves and land planted as much cotton as possible, so slave labor was in even greater demand than before. Slaves might have to pick from dawn to dusk, and the shells of the cotton blistered their fingers. Plantation owners who needed more workers bought more and more slaves as their work load increased. The slaves planted, harvested, cared for crops, did laundry, and cooked. Meanwhile, the owners were free to do other things and make money from the sweat of their slaves.

Life was hard for the slaves on the plantations. They had to work in the hot sun, from sunup to sundown. They had to stay on the plantation, and it became their world. They lost all the things they had once known—their culture, their language, their families, and their freedom. Even the weather and climate were different from Africa.

Slaves were often treated badly. We heard of one slave owner who whipped his slave to death because he called him "mister" instead of "master." Another slave was whipped because he looked at the dead slave and started to cry. If slaves were caught trying to escape, they were severely punished by whipping, jail, or death. Most slave owners— or masters, as they were called—didn't want to execute their slaves because slaves were considered valuable property. When slaves were lucky enough to escape, they had little chance of freedom. Their skin color made them easily identifiable.

Although many slaves were treated poorly, they brought many wonderful things to America with them. The slaves knew how to plant the crops and when to harvest them, because they did this according to a solar calendar in Africa. Blacks were creative and talented. Many of them were good woodcarvers, basket makers, weavers, potters, iron workers, and chemists.

The "underground railroad" helped many black slaves to freedom. Freedom meant going where slavery was illegal— the free states, the northern or western territories, or Canada. The so-called railroad started near the middle of the 1800s. In 1830, a slave named Tice

Davids escaped from his Kentucky owner. Tice swam across a river in sight of his owner and disappeared on the other side. The owner said he must have taken an underground road. Slaves heard about Tice Davids and later, when other slaves would escape, they were said to have used the "underground railroad."

But there was never an actual underground railroad system. It was called "underground" because it was hidden and "railroad" because it transported people. The underground railroad was made up of a group of people who helped slaves get to a free place to live. People who felt that slavery was wrong hid runaway slaves in their homes and farms, even though it could get them in trouble. Sometimes people had passages in their houses with walls that would move so that slaves could hide behind them. Many people who were against slavery used their homes as stops on the underground railroad.

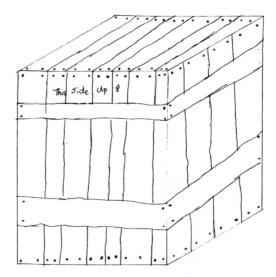

These houses were called "stations." "Stationmasters" were the owners of the houses and other hiding places. The slaves were called "passengers." One slave named Hezekiah Hill hid for a year under the floor of a stationmaster's house before his friend could get a boat and take him to freedom. A slave named Henry Hill used an unusual way to escape. He put himself in a box and mailed himself north to freedom, earning the nickname "Box."

EMANCIPATION

In 1865, the Civil War ended, and the underground railroad finally stopped running. The Civil War brought an official end to slavery and put America on the road to racial equality. A group of white and black people called abolition-

President Abraham Lincoln delivered the Emancipation Proclamation in 1862.

ists were active in many cities, mostly in the North. They drew up petitions against slavery and gave them to their leaders in Congress. Some worked hard to help free black people in their towns and cities.

Harriet Tubman, Frederick Douglass, and Sojourner Truth were African American leaders of the abolitionists in the 1800s. They were brave because they spoke up for African American rights during a time in America when blacks had few rights and little freedom.

During the Civil War, the South fought to keep slavery. To make money, plantation owners needed many people to work for little or nothing. The northern states had a different economy and didn't need slaves. They built factories, using machines and natural resources. When the North put an end to slavery, many factories and businesses hired blacks to work as cheap labor.

Do you know who the Great Emancipator was? He was President Abraham Lincoln, and he delivered the speech known as the Emancipation Proclamation in 1862. To emancipate means to set free from an influence or authority. A proclamation is an official public announcement. The Emancipation Proclamation was important because it helped end slavery in the United States.

The Civil War was still being fought when Lincoln issued the Emancipation Proclamation. Many things didn't change for those on the Union (the North) side because they were already free. In fact, it freed no one right away, but it had a great effect in the long run. Runaway slaves moved to northern states and to Canada. Though it made the South angry, it improved the image of the Union in Europe, because people there now believed slavery was wrong. Although the Emancipation Proclamation didn't officially end slavery in America, on December 18, 1865—after the Civil War—the 13th amendment to the

The Emancipation Proclamation was the official announcement that led to the end of slavery in the United States.

Constitution did. "Neither slavery nor involuntary servitude," it said, "except as a punishment for a crime whereof the party shall have been duly convicted, shall exist within the U.S."

By the end of the Civil War, about 180,000 blacks were fighting in Lincoln's Union army and about 30,000 in the Union navy. Thirty-eight thousand blacks died fighting for the Union cause —the cause of freedom.

RECONSTRUCTION

After the Civil War, the South was in terrible condition because that's where most of the fiercest battles had been fought. The North was in excellent shape because it had factories, farms, and railroads, all of which were developed even more in the war effort.

Reconstruction was the time in United States history that followed the Civil War. It was when the North and South finally made peace with each other. It was a time to rebuild the South and a time to heal the hard feelings in the country. This period in history (1865–1877) gave African Americans some of the freedom and rights they deserved. However, many African Americans discovered they had freedom but little else. They had no land, no money, and no means to live. Some worked on the same land that they had worked on as slaves, only now they worked as sharecroppers. Sharecroppers could grow crops and share the profits with the landowners. Many blacks moved North to the cities, looking for work and a better life. Unfortunately, many ended up living in poverty in the new ghettos with other immigrant groups and ethnic minorities. They often lived in poor housing, had low-paying jobs, and paid high prices for food and clothing.

Reconstruction solved many problems between the North and the South, which decided to join together again as the United States of America to build one strong nation. Congress passed laws to protect African Americans and gave them the right to vote. But other problems still remained. Most southern whites still didn't accept African Americans as equals. Living and working conditions hadn't improved much for African Americans. Pretty soon, the North seemed to forget about Reconstruction, and southern whites ignored many of the rights the African Americans had won earlier. To some whites in the South, slavery was necessary for their way of life. Blacks were kept from voting by the use of violence, voting taxes, and other discriminatory practices. The Ku Klux Klan (KKK) was founded at this time, and its members beat and murdered blacks and their white supporters. Reconstruction didn't solve the problems of prejudice in America.

THE ROAD TO FREEDOM

Another important period of time in U.S. history centers around the civil rights movement. Civil rights make sure people have their freedom and enable them to participate in society equally. Going places that you choose, sitting where you want, saying what you believe, and going to any school you choose are all examples of civil rights. This makes all people more respectful of other races and cultures. Many events in U.S. history following the Civil War encouraged everyone to get along better.

In Niagara Falls, New York, W. E. B. Du Bois called a meeting so that African Americans could talk about how to deal with their unequal treatment. It was called the Niagara Movement. It was a gathering of black scholars who felt that first-class citizenship should be guaranteed to all blacks. Not everyone who attended agreed with Du Bois, but the group did make a list of changes that needed to be made. Started in 1905, the movement lasted only four years before it ran out of money.

In 1910, Du Bois again tried to organize African Americans. He started the National Association for the Advancement of Colored People (NAACP) with some of the people from the Niagara Movement and some whites. The NAACP became the number one organization with the knowledge and the money to fight for justice for black Americans. The NAACP was very active during the years that Martin Luther King Jr. was working for racial equality. The organization still provides legal help for black people with problems that affect their community or themselves as individuals. They raise money through donations from concerned people.

In 1911, the National Urban League was founded by Booker T. Washington in New York City. He disagreed with Du Bois about how to help blacks. Du Bois thought heritage was most important, and Washington thought jobs were most

W. E. B. Du Bois was a scholar, writer, and leader for black rights in the early 1900s.

important. Today, the National Urban League is still helping African Americans find jobs and housing as well as giving them emotional support in big cities.

In the twentieth century, black people first began to make cultural advancements during the Harlem Renaissance, which began in 1912 in a section of New York City. This was an important time in black culture, because America began to show a growing appreciation for the work of black artists. During this time, black artists in art, music, and dance knew this was their chance to teach white people more about black culture. However, though blacks were being recognized for their artistic accomplishments, they still faced discrimination and problems at work.

In 1919, Samuel Gompers started the American Federation of Labor because he said he wanted to end discrimination against all people in the workplace. Since Gompers couldn't end discrimination all by himself, other people helped. A. Philip Randolph had the goal of getting better working conditions for the many black people who worked for the Pullman Company. They wanted more money, a shorter work week, and equal treatment. Randolph tripled the number of black people working for the Pullman Company. He told people to go in and tell their bosses to give them what they wanted. Black employees said they wouldn't work if they didn't get better working conditions. The workers wanted to prove that the company needed them

by showing what it would be like if no one did their jobs—if they went on strike. This plan eventually worked. They received a contract that improved their working conditions and also doubled, then tripled, their weekly pay.

In 1929, the Great Depression began. It lasted through the 1930s. During this time, many people of all races were without jobs, money, and food. President Franklin D. Roosevelt wanted to relieve the hunger and poverty of all people, and he was opposed to racial discrimination.

Mary McLeod Bethune, a black woman, was named the head of the National Youth Organization of Concern by President Roosevelt. This organization gave money to college students to continue their education. Mrs. Bethune was very active in civil rights issues. She founded the National Council of Negro Women, a group that helped black people with social, economic, and political concerns. Mrs. Bethune and Mrs. Roosevelt were very good friends. Mrs. Bethune was the first black woman to have an official job advising the president.

After the Depression, people were still angry that African Americans didn't have equal rights. Have you ever been so angry at something that you wanted to walk to the White House and let the President know how mad you were? Blacks and whites in 1941 decided they were fed up with discrimination. Thousands of people threatened to march on Washington to end discrimination in the defense industry, which was building weapons, ships, and planes for the military. Black leaders such as A. Philip Randolph and Bayard Rustin planned the march. Fortunately, the rally never took place because President Roosevelt jumped in and assured people that he would end discrimination in the government.

What did more than a million African Americans feel like as they were fighting World War II, when the armed forces were still segregated? Black servicemen hated it as much as those blacks who weren't in the military. Most

Military units were segregated during World War II.

blacks in the air force were maintenance workers because they weren't allowed to become pilots until a black training center was opened in Tuskegee, Alabama, in 1942. In the navy, most blacks were cooks until 1945, when they were allowed to become officers. In the army, as well as in other services, blacks were kept together as whole units. Some black units such as the 99th Pursuit Air Force Squadron and the 761st Army Tank Battalion fought heroically. In 1948, after the war ended, William Hastie, A. Philip Randolph, and Thurgood Marshall worked toward having the armed forces desegregated. They

told the black men not to enlist in the military if everything was still segregated. Harry Truman, who was President at the time, wanted black men in the military, so he issued an order that guaranteed equal treatment and equal opportunity for African Americans in the armed forces.

One very important event in the civil rights movement took place in 1954, when the case of *Brown v. Board of Education of Topeka, Kansas,* went to court. This was a case arguing that black and white kids should be allowed to go to the same schools. Black children didn't like going to separate schools because most white schools had more books and better teachers and facilities. Often, blacks had to travel farther to go to all-black schools. For two years, *Brown v. Board of Education* was heard in several courts. The last was the U.S. Supreme Court, and their decision was to desegregate all public schools. Even though this meant going where they weren't wanted, black people were pleased with the decision.

One of the most important persons in the civil rights movement was Reverend Dr. Martin Luther King Jr. the followers of Dr. King used nonviolent ways to get their ideas across. On December 1, 1955, someone decided to take a stand against the white belief that black people weren't as good as white people. Many racial practices in America at that time were known as "Jim Crow laws." They might seem silly now, but they really existed then. Throughout the South, blacks had to use different bathrooms, schools, and drinking fountains. Signs read "White Only" and "Colored Only," and many businesses refused to serve blacks. Blacks had to sit in the backs of buses and in different sections of restaurants. They received their wages from different pay windows. There was even a rule that black and white cotton-mill workers couldn't look out the same window. Some unfair racial practices were just as common in the northern states, but without posted signs.

Then one cold December day, on a bus in Montgomery, Alabama, a woman

named Rosa Parks decided to fight for her civil rights.

If the white section of a bus in the South became full, then black people in the back of the bus had to give up their seats. Rosa Parks refused to give up her seat, so she was arrested. This event led to the Montgomery Bus Boycott.

The Montgomery Bus Boycott was led by E. D. Nixon. Mr. Nixon passed out leaflets urging all blacks not to ride on the buses. The boycott was announced in Sunday church services and newspapers. This was hard for some blacks to do because the bus was their only way to get to work. Many people couldn't afford to miss work and lose a day's pay. Some people ended up carpooling or

Reverend Dr. Martin Luther King Jr. was a civil rights leader whose philosophy of nonviolence inspired generations of Americans.

even riding mules. Some walked many miles to work.

Normally the buses were crowded, but on the first day of the boycott, there were hardly any blacks on any bus in the city. Nixon called a community meeting at a local church. So many people came that they had to sit outside on the lawn and listen through speakers. Nixon suggested that they boycott all buses in the South until they were desegregated. Then Reverend Dr. Martin Luther King Jr. stood up and gave a speech telling the people that it was time to stop letting other people keep them from being free. His speech was so powerful that the quiet, calm crowd burst into standing ovations.

Martin Luther King Jr. is the most famous and respected civil rights leader in America. He did many things to help all people become sensitive about other cultures and races. Many civil rights organizations have used his model of nonviolence in an effort to try to achieve a better way of life. Dr. King believed strongly in the power of peace-

ful protests (such as organized boycotts and sit-ins) instead of violence. Even today, many groups use his methods of peaceful protest to make positive social and political changes.

Lots of publicity surrounded the Montgomery boycott, and southern blacks decided to work for even more rights. They started holding sit-ins and rallies to show that they wouldn't accept segregation or Jim Crow laws any longer. Freedom riders—people sworn to nonviolence—took "freedom rides" to make sure that bus, air, and rail lines were desegregated. Everywhere the freedom riders went, they were met with violence. Mobs of racists beat people, burned buses, and terrorized black and white freedom riders. Sometimes, police and National Guard troops didn't do anything to stop the violence that was going on right in front of them. Even ambulance drivers and hospitals in the area sometimes didn't do anything to help injured protestors. Many protestors were permanently disabled or killed during the riots. The problem got so bad that President John F. Kennedy and his brother Robert Kennedy—who was attorney general of the United States—had to step in to try to stop the violence. They ordered the governors of Alabama and Mississippi to cooperate with the freedom riders, but the governors didn't listen. They allowed the police to beat and arrest the freedom riders. President Kennedy recommended that blacks vote in great numbers so that the prejudiced sheriffs and judges who allowed segregation could be voted out of office. This often worked, and the buses were eventually desegregated.

The year 1963 was a hard one for Martin Luther King Jr. and his followers. All over the country there were strong racist feelings. In Alabama, George Wallace was elected governor because he said that there would be no integration in Alabama, ever. As a result, public places like swimming pools, parks, playgrounds, and golf courses were closed down just to keep blacks out. So Dr. King decided to make Birmingham, Alabama, the next target of his protests against segregation. Fifteen thousand of Dr. King's supporters were arrested for protesting, even though they were peaceful. Even some 6-year-old children were arrested.

Boycotts and sit-ins were powerful peaceful protests.

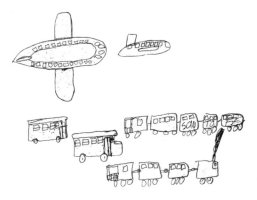

By the summer of 1963, blacks were demanding full equality. Many black organizations chose August 28 for a march on Washington, D.C. The leaders of the march expected only a few thousand people to attend. Instead, more than 300,000 people came. Two thousand freedom buses and 30 freedom trains from all over the country brought black people to Washington, D.C. Hour after hour, people arrived at the Lincoln Memorial. The entire area between the Washington Monument and the Lincoln Memorial became a sea of people, black and white, fighting against prejudice together. At the time, it was the largest demonstration ever held in the United States. It was at this march that Martin Luther King Jr. gave his famous "I Have a Dream" speech.

Martin Luther King Jr. wasn't the only civil rights leader. The Black Power Movement also fought for civil rights, but it wasn't as peaceful as Dr. King. They didn't want to wait for things to happen. They wanted to force changes immediately.

One of the people involved in the Black Power Movement was Malcolm X. Malcolm changed his last name from "Little" to "X" because he didn't like the fact that the name "Little" had been given to his family by slave masters. He said that the X represented his unknown black ancestry. When he was a young person, Malcolm quit school and became a criminal. He was arrested when he was a teenager. When he was in jail, he read a lot about freedom and started to work toward freedom for blacks. He also became a follower of Elijah Muhammad, the leader of the Black Muslim church in America. When he got out of jail, he worked with Muhammad as an assistant minister. Soon, Muhammad appointed Malcolm as his national minister. Other Muslims became jealous of him, and Malcolm began to suspect his enemies were turning Muhammad against him. Soon, Malcolm and other members of the Black Muslims, including Muhammad, began to disagree about how to handle certain situations. In 1964, Malcolm announced he was leaving the group. He started a new group, the Organization for Afro-American Unity. Malcolm was known for his strong ideas and for being outspoken. In 1965, he was assassinated, but his memory is still alive in the fight for equality.

Another group that was part of the Black Power Movement was the Black Panthers. This group opened their own schools to educate people about black heritage. They organized food distribu-

In the summer of 1963, 300,000 people attended the March on Washington for People's Rights.

Malcolm X was an important spokesman for equal rights.

tion centers for the poor. They also educated people about their rights. The Black Panthers were people who didn't mind doing violent things to gain civil rights. One of the things they would do was to follow police cars and see if they were going to stop any black people and pick on them. If they thought the police stopped a black person unjustly, the Black Panthers would get out of their cars and get involved. The police wanted to pass a law so the Black Panthers couldn't carry guns. The day that the government was going to decide about the issue, some Black Panthers went to the meeting and spoke about their beliefs and rights. Even though the Black Panthers told the court that they had done nothing wrong, they were arrested and sent to jail for six months.

A UCLA professor named Angela Davis was a member of the Black Panthers. She was in charge of political education. She went around talking about rights that black people should have. She was especially interested in the case of three black prisoners. These men had been accused of murdering a guard at Soledad Prison. She thought this was unfair because there was no proof that they were involved in the crime. Jonathan Jackson, the brother of one of the prisoners, kidnapped the judge, district attorney, and several jurors during the trial of the three men. He said that if they didn't free his brother, he would kill his hostages. When Jonathan Jackson and the hostages got to the van, a bunch of shots hit the van, and some of the people he kidnapped were dead. The police

Angela Davis was an educator and a Black Power Movement leader for the Black Panthers.

never found out who fired the shots, but Angela Davis was arrested because she was the one accused of owning the guns used in the kidnapping. The charges were dismissed in July 1972.

LIVING THROUGH HISTORY: CARLOTTA WALLS LaNIER

History books are filled with famous names, places, and events. Have you ever wanted to find out what it was really like back then? We'll never forget the day we had the opportunity to get to know Carlotta Walls LaNier. Now she is more than a name in a history book to us. We want to share with you the story of this courageous woman who lived through an important time in our country's history. She didn't try to make history, she just did. When the time came, she did what was right.

Can you imagine what it would be like to really change things in your own school? What about changing things in schools all across America? In the 1950s, Carlotta Walls LaNier was one of the "Little Rock Nine"—nine high-school students who challenged the way America treated black people. We tried to put ourselves in her shoes. What would it be like to do what she did? What would our schools be like today if she hadn't been willing to do what was right? Mrs. LaNier taught us to think about our choices and to be willing to meet the challenges in the future. Someday we might be called upon to change some-

Carlotta Walls LaNier

thing in our country's future. We can use Mrs. Lanier as an example of how to act.

In the spring of 1956, Carlotta Walls was a ninth grader at a junior high school for African American students in Little Rock, Arkansas. "If you live near Central High and would like to go there next fall," the teacher had said, "just sign your name and pass it on." The thought of being able to attend Central High excited Carlotta. Her mother had told her over and over that education was the road to success. This was a chance to get the same education as white children, and the school was only three miles from her house. Dunbar High

School was for blacks only, and it was 12 miles away. Young Carlotta carefully signed the piece of paper and passed it on. Little did she know that she would soon have a part in changing American history forever.

In 1954, the U.S. Supreme Court decided that African Americans—called coloreds, blacks, or Negroes back then—were to be treated the same as other people. Before that decision, colored and white people were treated very differently. For example, blacks couldn't try on clothes in any of the stores. They just had to buy the clothes, shoes, or hats and take them home. If they didn't fit, they couldn't take the clothes back.

Most of the schools for black students never got enough money to buy new books or school equipment. When the white schools received money to buy new books, their old ones were sent to schools like the one young Carlotta attended. She knew she would learn a lot more at Little Rock Central High School. She couldn't help but learn more with all those new books and real equipment in the science lab! She hoped the new school would set her on the road to a successful life.

Seventy-two African American students signed up to go to Central High, but when school opened, only nine were brave enough to show up. That's why they were later called "The Little Rock Nine." The adults thought it would be safer if all the black students went in together, but Elizabeth Eckford was miss-ing. Where was she? They looked and looked, but finally decided to go in without her since they didn't want to be late on their first day. As they walked toward the door of the school, there were angry crowds of white people yelling bad names and throwing rocks at them. The nine students were glad to see that Governor Faubus had sent the National Guard to protect them, just as he had promised the night before. But much to their surprise, when they got to the door, the National Guard members crossed their bayonets and shouted, "Leave! Leave now!"

Meanwhile, Elizabeth was at the other end of the very large school. She couldn't find her friends anywhere. She was surrounded by a mob screaming names and throwing rocks at her. She was nervous and scared. Really scared! Luckily, a woman named Gladys Lorch and a reporter, Benjamin Fine, surrounded her and helped her onto the bus, where her friends were waiting. All the African American students were taken back to their homes.

Governor Faubus said that the federal government couldn't make the laws for Arkansas because Arkansas didn't want any blacks in the white schools. The Little Rock Nine were not allowed to go back to school for a long time. They were angry that the white children were learning while they had to sit at home. Finally, after three weeks, the teachers began sending work home for the students to do. In spite of the Supreme Court, Governor Faubus still refused to let the African American students go to Central High. The students were proud that Thurgood Marshall Jr. was arguing their case in court. They were anxious to go back to school.

During that time, Governor Faubus had a meeting with President Eisenhower. The president said that Arkansas had to obey the Supreme Court's decision and let the Nine go to Central High. People thought that the governor had finally agreed to do the right thing. On Monday, the Nine went back to Central High, but they left quickly when an angry mob stormed the school. Carlotta remembers it as "the most frightening day." Governor Faubus had disobeyed the president and broken the law. He had removed the National Guard and left the police to handle all the problems. Even police officers were being hurt! In November, President Eisenhower sent guards from the 101st Airborne to Little Rock Central High School to protect the black students and let them go to school. Some thought Eisenhower was a hero, but Carlotta wondered what had taken him so long.

The white guards walked them to the door of their class and stood outside

U.S. troops desegregate Little Rock Central High School.

until class was over. These African American students had been active in their own school and had brought their wonderful talents with them. They wanted to be involved in everything in their new school, but found out that they couldn't participate in band, choir, yearbook, newspaper, track, or the student council. School became a job for them—it was no fun.

All sorts of things happened to the Nine. They learned to do their work and to not ask questions if their grades went down in some classes. Gym class was one of the worst because it was just too hard to keep an eye on all of the kids. Sometimes when they took a shower, someone would turn off the cold water, and the hot water would scar their skin. Terrance, one of the Nine, even got stabbed in the leg. They always kept extra clothes with them so they could change if they had raw eggs thrown at them. Ink was spilled on their chairs, and food was dropped on them.

Even with guards, these students had to put up with abuse every day. They were called ugly names and were kicked and tripped in the hallway. Their books were stolen, and their lockers were broken into. Carlotta walked fast so that kids wouldn't step on the back of her heels. She felt that if they were going to hurt her, they were going to have to work hard to do it. She became known as the "Road Runner." It didn't help to tell the vice-principal or teachers about their problems—they would just smile and do nothing.

In spite of the terrible things that happened to her and her family, Carlotta graduated from Little Rock Central High School in 1960. She gives her parents a lot of credit for their courage in supporting her. Her father lost many jobs when people found out that his daughter was one of the students "causing all that trouble" at Little Rock Central High School. He was worried about his daughter, but he never told her to quit school, even when his home was bombed on February 9, 1960. After the bombing, Carlotta's father was the first one taken to jail and questioned by the police for 72 hours.

It was hard for the Little Rock Nine to put up with all the problems. We're glad that they had the courage to do it because they changed history for the better. Mrs. LaNier is concerned that what happened to the Nine might happen again if people don't respect one another. She believes that having kids from different cultural backgrounds get a good education is important.

Mrs. LaNier graduated from the University of Northern Colorado with a degree in recreation administration and social studies. She has been a YWCA administrator and a realtor. She is a Board Member for the Colorado AIDS Project and is on the Board of Trustees for Park Hill United Methodist Church. Mrs. LaNier was given the Spingarn Medal by the National Association for the Advancement of Colored People (NAACP) for her courage in Little Rock.

Whether she is at home or at work,

Mrs. LaNier often thinks about what happened back in 1956 and 1957. She knows she did the right thing, and she would do it all over again if she had to, even though she didn't realize that it would become such a significant event in America's history. She reminded us that it is everyone's job to do their best to do the right thing. You never know— you might just change history.

AMERICA TODAY

Much has aided the progress of African Americans in America. Peaceful protests, political reforms, education, and better jobs have all helped. The civil rights battle opened the doors of opportunity for many African Americans, but it still left our country with racial problems and injustices. Education is the real key to changing people's attitudes and their positions in society. Overall, education has improved in the African American community, although we are still working toward equality.

African American groups and educational systems all across America have been alarmed at the high rate of minorities dropping out of schools. In the 1990s, people have continued to look for reasons why many schools are not meeting the cultural and social needs of black students. One problem is that there are very few role models for African American students within the schools. Only 8 percent of teachers in America are African Americans. Because there are so few black teachers, many teachers find it difficult to reach their students on a personal level. Money has been another problem, and schools are struggling financially. Researchers found that even schools having a majority of black students don't provide many special programs for them.

Without a good education, many young men are turning to crime and being killed in gangs and drug deals. Because of these problems, leaders are trying to change things in our schools to encourage more black young men to go to college so they can get good jobs. School systems throughout the U.S. are designing special programs meant to help African Americans deal with their lives and get a better education. For example, in Detroit, Michigan, the Board of Education set up a special school for kids in kindergarten through the eighth grade. This school is designed for African American boys only. They are hoping to better help the emotional, social, and educational needs of these students. In Baltimore, Maryland, Coleman Elementary has all-male and all-female classrooms and works hard to address problems like drug dealers in the kids' neighborhoods and low test scores. When this program first started, Coleman was just another troubled school in an all-black neighborhood. A few years later, students at Coleman scored within the top five elementary schools in their city on standardized tests.

Right now, there are many groups using legal and political means to work for positive change for black Americans. Groups working for affirmative action have helped minorities get better jobs, access to more schools and universities, and legal rights that weren't theirs before. Affirmative action is a program that helps minority groups have better chances for jobs and an education by persuading the government to pass fairer laws. Some groups working on this problem feel the United States has a culture that enables only white people to get ahead in life. These people have worked for affirmative-action programs that benefit African Americans and other minorities, including women and people with disabilities.

In 1995, California universities decided not to have different standards for minority student admissions, because some people feel that these affirmative-action programs are examples of reverse discrimination. Many others disagree with these changes in affirmative action. They want to increase the minority enrollment in college because they believe that all students need a good education in order for our country to be strong and prosperous.

African American organizations are assisting young black students by creating scholarships and grants to help them pay for their education. These scholarships benefit interested and smart students throughout the United States. Another way education is changing is that many schools are starting to offer black studies programs. Temple University in Philadelphia was the first college to establish a doctoral program in African American studies.

The United Negro College Fund (UNCF) also works to help black students get an education. This is a non-profit, fund-raising association for 41 of the largest black colleges in the United States. Its members include 39 private colleges and universities and two graduate schools. The motto of the UNCF is "A mind is a terrible thing to waste," which means we need to provide a chance for all people to get an education. Education puts more people into the scientific, medical, and business fields, and it creates a better society for all of us. We need as many people working toward the growth of our country as possible.

Education is not the only challenge facing African Americans today. There are still the problems of poverty, violence, and racism. Poverty can be found in any black neighborhood and in any city or town in this country. This is a very big problem because joblessness and a lack of opportunities can lead to frustration and violence.

Some people believe that violence comes from anger when people cannot control their own lives. Name-calling and beatings are signs of a war between races that may never end. Leaders and their followers are trying to stop this war. Some have died while fighting, and some have lived to tell their story. In 1991, for example, a black man named Rodney King was arrested for reckless driving and was beaten up by the police in Los Angeles. Another man happened to videotape the whole thing. The police officers who beat Rodney King were taken to court in 1992. The jury found them not guilty because the police said that Mr. King was resisting arrest. Many people in our nation were upset about this. It was a scary time.

There were disturbances and riots in several places across our country, but those in Los Angeles were the worst. Some people, who were angry that the police beat Rodney King, went out and beat up other people and burned down dozens of businesses in the Los Angeles area. Other people broke into stores and stole things. Rodney King asked people to stop acting this way. He told them that we all have to learn to get along. Throughout the riot, all races were involved in the fighting. But afterward, people of all races were involved in cleaning up the devastation from the riots.

There are still many problems with racism in the United States. Thanks to some people, equal rights laws have been passed. Blacks have more opportunities for employment and advancement, and they have a better chance to get an education beyond high school. In politics, African American people have run for public offices such as governor, mayor, even president. Shirley Chisholm

was the first black *and* the first woman to run for president in the 1970s. Jesse Jackson ran for president in 1988. In 1990, Douglas Wilder became the first African American governor in the history of the United States. Wellington Web was elected mayor of Denver, Colorado, in 1991. His opponent was also black. In the November 1992 election in Illinois, Carol Moseley Braun became the United States' first black woman senator. In 1991, then-President Bush nominated Clarence Thomas, an African American judge, to be a member of the U.S. Supreme Court. When President Clinton was elected in 1992, he chose seven African Americans for his cabinet, to give him advice and help him with decisions. In the 1994 election, 39 African Americans continued as, or became members of, the United States Senate and House of Representatives. More are being elected every year.

As more black Americans take leadership roles in government, we know they will continue to make good things happen for our country. We hope that the programs and groups working today can continue to make positive changes, such as when President Reagan signed a law that set aside the third Monday of January as a day to honor Martin Luther King Jr. By 1993, every state celebrated this day as a special holiday. It feels good to know that this is one of the changes and celebrations of the African American culture and heritage. It is our hope that with time and effort, many more of these important gains will pull our communities together, just as Martin Luther King wanted.

Some of the protests in the last 20 years have been successful in making a statement about fairness for all races. Others were not so successful but have made a mark for people to remember. At least people across our nation recognize we still have a problem with racism and equality. Together we can do away with racism and prejudice.

We hope to see a future with fairness for African Americans and people of all races. We hope to have more and better jobs for all people, so that they can take care of themselves and live a better life. We hope that this book will help make people of all races understand that everyone is equal.

FAMOUS FIRSTS AND HEROES

The battles they have fought
Have given us a lot.
Always working at their best,
They tried hard to pass the test.

Americans have suffered, worked, and grown stronger throughout the history of America. They have used determination, strength, and wisdom to overcome problems. They've helped the United States by improving their own lives as well as the lives of others. For example, their long struggle for civil rights has resulted in laws to end discrimination against all races, religions, and cultures. These laws guarantee the right to vote and other rights to all U.S. citizens.

In this chapter, we will tell you about people who became famous by being the first to accomplish important things. We call these people "famous firsts." We also write about some out-standing heroes among the African American people. They are civil-rights leaders, inventors, scientists, doctors, educators, religious leaders, people in government, explorers, athletes, and others. We'll discuss African Americans who are well-known and some African Americans most of us have never heard of.

We have chosen to write about 12 people in greater depth. These people are arranged in order by the year in which they were born. This helped us see which people were alive at the same time and when they made their contributions. There are so many people to write about that it was difficult to choose. We have left out some of the most famous heroes because you can read about them in other sections of our book. For example, you will find out about George Washington Carver and Mary McLeod Bethune in the food section. We hope that you will go to the library and do research on more great African Americans. If it weren't for people like these, the world would be a different place today.

FEATURED BIOGRAPHIES

Lucy Terry Prince (1730–1821)

Lucy Terry Prince was the first recognized African American poet and a fighter for the rights of African Americans.

Lucy was captured in Africa at the age of five, brought to this country, and sold to a couple in Deerfield, Massachusetts. At age 16, Lucy was serving as a nurse when Indians attacked Deerfield. What happened affected her so much that she wrote a poem based on the Indian attack. Her poem was called "The Bar's Fight."

Later, Lucy met her husband-to-be, Abijah Prince. He had been a slave who fought in the militia during the French and Indian War. Mr. Prince was given his freedom and three very valuable pieces of land in Northfield, Massachusetts.

Mr. Prince bought Lucy's freedom from her owners, and in 1756, they were married and moved to Guilford, Vermont, where he had been given a 100-acre farm by his employer. After a few years, one of their neighbors tried to claim the couple's farm. Lucy Terry Prince rode to the city and told the

governor's council. The council heard Ms. Prince's complaint and ruled in her favor. Ms. Prince returned home feeling good, because never before in American history had an African American woman been able to get the attention of such high officials and achieve that much success.

But Lucy Prince became frustrated when she tried to enter her youngest son, Abijah Jr., in the new Williams College. No matter what the Princes tried, the officials at Williams College wouldn't let him attend. Ms. Prince and her family continued to go on in spite of this setback. Later, when her husband died, one of Ms. Prince's white neighbors wanted some of the Prince property in Sunderland. Ms. Prince again fought to keep all her land by going to court. The Vermont Supreme Court heard Ms. Prince's argument and once again ruled in her favor.

Benjamin Banneker (1731–1806)

Benjamin Banneker was the first African American astronomer, mathematician, and surveyor. He was also an inventor. Mr. Banneker was born on November 9, 1731, in Baltimore, Maryland. He came into this world like every African American should have—free. His grandmother came from England, and she taught Benjamin to read, write, and do arithmetic. He would count caterpillars, weeds, stars, and even tobacco seeds. When he was 12 years old, he went to a nearby Quaker school. Learning was very easy for Benjamin, and he especially loved science and math.

When he was only 21, Mr. Banneker made the first clock that chimed every hour. It was made completely of wood, including the gears, which he carved with a knife. He learned how to make the clock from a watch that he had borrowed, taken apart, studied, and

then put back together in perfect condition. Mr. Banneker's clock kept perfect time for 40 years.

After making the striking clock, Benjamin borrowed books on astronomy, the study of stars and planets. He studied until he knew all there was to know about astronomy. He correctly predicted a solar eclipse in 1789. For ten years, he made all the calculations to predict the movements of the stars and tides and wrote a yearly almanac. An almanac is a book that tells facts and makes predictions about the stars, moon, planets, tides, and weather. This almanac was the first scientific book written by an African American. Mr. Banneker continued to work and study, becoming an expert in surveying (measuring land for mapmakers and builders) as well as astronomy and mathematics.

In 1791, President George Washington asked Mr. Banneker to help plan the streets and buildings in Washington, D.C. He was the first African American to be asked to do a job by a U.S. President. Mr. Banneker also wrote a plan for world peace, which was the model used 100 years later for the League of Nations' plan proposed by President Woodrow Wilson. He worked for world peace and freedom for all people.

Benjamin Banneker also spoke out strongly against slavery and in favor of free public education for all children, black and white. He wrote a letter about this to Thomas Jefferson, who was so impressed that he sent Mr. Banneker's almanac to the Royal Academy of Sciences in Paris. With all his accomplishments, Benjamin Banneker proved wrong those people who believed that African Americans were not intelligent or capable of learning.

Bill Pickett (1860–1932)

Bill Pickett was one of the West's most exciting cowboys. This tall black cowboy thrilled the crowd with his bulldogging ability. Bulldogging is when a cowboy grabs a bull by the horns, twists its head, and forces it over on its side. Mr. Pickett was courageous and strong. After he threw the bull to the ground, he would stare the bull right in the eye. This usually scared the bull so much that it wouldn't charge at him.

When he was 40, Mr. Pickett went to work for a ranch in Oklahoma called the 101 Ranch. All of the cowhands there did something special. Will Rogers did wonderful rope tricks, Tom Mix was

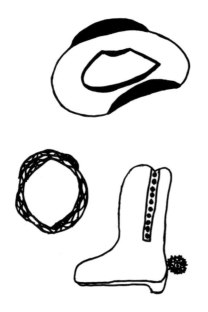

a fine horseman, and Bill Pickett was the best bulldogger people had ever seen. He handled horses with great skill and was a very tough man who loved the cowboy way of life. The cowhands took their 101 Ranch Rodeo Show to famous Madison Square Garden in New York City. On opening night, a wild steer got loose and ran into the stands where the people were sitting. Will Rogers roped the steer, and Bill Pickett hung onto the bull's horns and pulled it back into the arena. The 101 Ranch Rodeo Show toured Mexico, Canada, and Europe. The crowds loved to see the famous African American bulldogger.

Bill Pickett was born in 1860 as a free man in the state of Texas. He died in 1932, after being trampled by a horse. Bill Pickett was honored as the first bulldogger in the Cowboy Hall of Fame.

Leroy B. "Satchel" Paige (1906–1987)

For 20 years, Leroy "Satchel" Paige was not allowed into baseball's white major leagues, even though he was an outstanding pitcher in the black leagues. In 1948, though, African Americans were finally allowed in the major leagues. Even though Mr. Paige was old for a baseball player, he still had a great pitching arm. No one knew exactly how old he was because he would never tell exactly what year he had been born. Some say he was more than 42 years old when he was signed by the Cleveland Indians.

Satchel Paige was a tall, thin man with very long arms that sometimes seemed to hang all the way down to his

knees. He often used a "windmill" windup, spinning his arm all the way around four or five times before letting go of the ball. On important pitches, he used a double windup, spinning his arm one way for a while and then stopping and spinning it the other, until he finally let go of the pitch. This drove both baseball fans and the opposing players crazy.

Newspaper reporters liked to interview Mr. Paige because he was kind of a philosopher, too.

"Satch, when they call you in from the bull pen," one reporter asked him, "why do you walk to the pitching mound so slowly?"

"When they calls me in to pitch," Satchel replied, "usually they's in some kind of trouble. Only a fool rushes into trouble."

One of Satchel's favorite sayings was,

"Don't never look back over your shoulder. Something might be gaining on you."

In 1971, Satchel Paige was elected into baseball's Hall of Fame as one of the greatest pitchers ever.

Thurgood Marshall (1908–1993)

Justice Marshall was the first African American to be appointed to the U.S. Supreme Court, the highest court in the land. When he was very young, his father taught him that not only did he have permission to fight, but he *should* fight to protect himself. It was this early advice that sometimes got Thurgood Marshall into trouble at school.

While he was in college, Mr. Marshall joined the debate team. He found that he was good at fighting with words. After thinking about it, he decided he would be a lawyer, because lawyers helped people by fighting with words.

The University of Maryland would

Justice Thurgood Marshall

not let him attend its law school because he was black, so he went to law school at Howard University, an African American university in Washington, D.C.

When he first became an attorney, Justice Marshall worked on cases that involved getting equal rights for African Americans. In 1936, he went to New York City to work for the NAACP (National Association for the Advancement of Colored People), to which both blacks and whites belonged. Two years later, he became the chief counsel for the NAACP, winning many cases for African American citizens. He fought for the laws that would give them the right to go to any college, attend the same public schools as white children, take any seat on a bus or train, register to vote, and sit down to eat at any restaurant.

Justice Marshall was nicknamed "Mr. Civil Rights." In 1961, President John F. Kennedy appointed him a federal judge. Some senators from the South didn't like this appointment. The Senate must approve any man named by the president as a federal judge. It took a year for the Senate to approve Justice Marshall. In 1965, President Lyndon B. Johnson appointed him solicitor general in the Department of Justice, the chief lawyer for the government. Finally, in 1967, President Johnson named Justice Marshall to the Supreme Court—the highest court in the United States. If you're on the Supreme Court, you're on it for life.

In 1991, Thurgood Marshall retired from the Supreme Court. Two years later—after a lifetime of working for civil rights—Justice Marshall died.

Jesse Owens (1913–1980)

"Ready, set, go!" shouted Jesse Owens' junior high coach. When the race was done, the coach looked at his stopwatch. "Wait a minute," he said to himself. "Does this watch say ten seconds?" He couldn't believe that Jesse Owens had just run the 100 yard dash in ten seconds. This was the beginning of an amazing story about an outstanding athlete.

Jesse Owens was an Olympic track star who left a huge mark on history and proved Adolf Hitler wrong. Hitler thought that the German people would win the Olympics because he said they were the master race. In 1936, the Olympics were held in Berlin. Mr. Owens set new Olympic records in the 100- and 200-meter sprints and the long jump, and he shared the world's record for the 400-meter relay. Hitler was really angry when Mr. Owens walked away with four gold medals, proving that it was his talent that made him a winner, not his nationality or skin color.

Jesse Owens was born September 12, 1913, in Oakville, Alabama. He was the son of a poor farming family. When he was seven years old, he and his family moved to Cleveland, Ohio. With the help of his junior-high coach, Jesse Owens became a high-school track star. He worked very hard in school, earning a scholarship to Ohio State University. There he broke world records in the long jump, hurdles, and running events.

During his life, Jesse Owens set seven world records.

To recognize Mr. Owens' many accomplishments during his lifetime, President Ford awarded him the Medal of Freedom in 1976. In 1979, President Carter gave him a Living Legends Award. Whenever Mr. Owens had a chance, he told young athletes to live good, healthy lives and to be honest. Jesse Owens died in 1980, but he will always be remembered for his outstanding ability and dedication.

Jackie Robinson (1919–1972)

Crack! went the ball on the bat. Off ran Jackie, the smallest kid and the best baseball player in the neighborhood. Jackie Robinson was a talented, determined, and disciplined man who became the first African American major-league baseball player. Jackie was born in a farmhouse on January 31, 1919, in Cairo, Georgia. He and his family moved to California. In the new neighborhood, they were the only black family on their block. Sometimes white neighbors were mean to them and even burned a cross on their front yard.

In school there were two baseball teams that played at recess and during lunch. Both teams wanted Jackie. He was very poor and wanted to save his mother the expense of giving him lunch, so he chose to play on any team that shared their lunches with him.

Jackie was an average student but a fabulous athlete. He was quick and competitive. Other players and coaches tried

to upset him, get him angry, and make him forget about the game by yelling racial remarks. But their remarks only made Jackie more determined to win.

One day, the phone rang at Mr. Robinson's home. The caller was Branch Rickey, the manager of the Brooklyn Dodgers. He invited Mr. Robinson to join the team. This was the first time a black baseball player had been invited to play in the majors. His first game was in 1947, and he hit a home run. Fans still yelled nasty comments and threw things at him, but through it all, he kept his temper. He knew that being the first black player wouldn't be easy, but he had the strength not to fight. In this way, he kept the door open for other blacks to play ball.

Mr. Robinson retired from baseball in 1957, but he kept himself busy. He became an active leader in the civil-rights movement, making speeches, and marching to gain equal rights for blacks. Five years after his retirement, he was elected into the Baseball Hall of Fame. On October 24, 1972, he died of a heart attack.

Jackie Robinson is considered one of America's greatest athletes, but he is also remembered for his courage—and his example. Today, millions of African American children dream of one day playing major league baseball.

Daniel "Chappie" James (1920–1978)

General Daniel James was the first African American four-star general. He was a well-respected leader, speaker, and war hero.

Daniel James was born in Florida in 1920. In 1942, he married Dorothy Watkins, and they had three children. Mr. James went to school at the Tuskegee Institute, where he majored in physical education. He also received civilian pilot training—training for those who aren't in the military. Thirty-two years after he entered the Army Air Corps Aviation Cadet Program, he became a four-star general. Throughout his army career, Mr. James worked in many areas of the United States as well as in other places around the world. He was in charge of many defense programs, which are programs set up to keep the United States safe.

Mr. James spent time in the Korean War as a fighter pilot. During the Korean War, he flew with a man named Robin Old. They went on so many missions together, that the other pilots nicknamed them Blackman and Robin, after the *Batman* television show. He also fought in the Vietnam War, where he was the second man in charge of a group of fighter planes.

Mr. James won more than 20 military awards, including the Distinguished Service Medal, the Distinguished Flying Cross, the Combat Readiness Medal, and the United Nations Service Medal. It's impressive that he received military awards for both wartime activities and peacetime activities, in addition to several community awards. He gave many speeches about the importance of respecting and loving America. He

General Daniel "Chappie" James

believed strongly in the "American Dream." Many people asked him to speak at their meetings or traveled from far away to hear his speeches.

General James retired from the U.S. Air Force in 1978 because something was wrong with his heart. Fifteen thousand people came to his retirement party. Sammy Davis Jr. brought his band and gave a two-hour concert. General James even got up and sang with him. A month later, he died from a heart attack.

Shirley Chisholm (b. 1924)

Shirley Chisholm was the first woman in the U.S. House of Representatives. She worked hard to obtain job training, higher education, and business counseling for black people. She strongly believed that these were the keys to a better life for African Americans.

Shirley's mother was a seamstress. Her father worked in a burlap factory. At an early age, she went to live with family members in Barbados in the West Indies, while her parents tried to save money for her education. Shirley returned to Brooklyn at age 11 and went to grade school and high school there. She earned college scholarships to Brooklyn College and Columbia University, where she earned a master's degree in elementary education. She worked as a nursery school teacher, managed a day-care center, and helped and advised the New York Department of Social Services. She became active in politics because the people in her neighborhood were looking for an honest, caring candidate.

Shirley Chisholm

While she was a representative, Ms. Chisholm sponsored the SEEK program, which offered minority students the chance to receive college-level classes, even if they hadn't graduated from high school. She also came up with the idea of a day-care program that would receive its money from public taxes, just as our public school system does.

Ms. Chisholm believed in using the information she learned in college and in her job. While she was in office, she worked only on projects she thought she knew about. One time, she was asked to work on an agriculture project. "Put me somewhere where I can use my talents and knowledge," she said. She was taken off that project and placed on another that she knew more about.

In 1972, Representative Chisholm announced that she wanted to run for president of the United States. It was unheard of at that time for any woman to run for president. But no one laughed. She was treated with the same consideration as the men running for this office. People respected her decision, and even if she didn't win, they still thought she was terrific.

Bill Cosby (b. 1937)

"Ha, ha, ha," laughs the audience listening to Bill Cosby on *The Cosby Show*. Mr. Cosby is a funny comedian. He has starred in shows such as *The Cosby Kids* and *I Spy*.

Mr. Cosby created and produced the cartoons *Fat Albert* and *The New Fat Albert Show* (1979–1984). He also hosted and did some of the voices on these shows. Both shows won many awards for their educational value. Bill Cosby is also a stand-up comedian. He has made up names like "Weird Harold" and "Crying Charlie" for his characters, but they are really based on the lives of his friends.

Bill Cosby was born on July 12, 1937, in Philadelphia, Pennsylvania. His dad left the family when Bill was eight, so he found a job shining shoes to make more money for his mom. Two years later, he got a job in a grocery store earning $8 a week. It bothered him that his mother had to work so hard to support the family. He promised her that someday she wouldn't have to work.

Bill Cosby

In high school, Mr. Cosby was the class clown. He failed most of his classes and eventually dropped out of school. In the navy, Mr. Cosby earned his high-school diploma. Later he enrolled at Temple University to become a gym teacher, but instead, he decided to be a comedian. Mr. Cosby never forgot that his mother wanted him to get an education. He received an honorary bachelor's degree from Temple, completing master's and doctorate degrees in education at the University of Massachusetts.

In 1964, Mr. Cosby married Camille. Today they have five children, named Erika, Erinn, Ennis, Ensa, and Evin. When asked why all of his children had names beginning with an "E," Bill

Cosby answers, "So they'll aim for excellence in their lives."

Arthur Ashe (1943–1993)

Arthur Ashe served the ball. Bang! Smash! Would you believe that anyone could hit a tennis ball over the net at 130 miles an hour? Arthur Ashe could. He could serve the ball harder than any other person in the tennis world. Arthur Ashe was the first African American to win the United States Open and Wimbledon tennis tournaments.

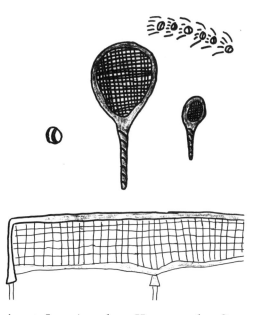

Mr. Ashe was born July 10, 1943. In the segregated city of Richmond, Virginia, where he grew up, little Arthur attended an all-black school. He had to drink from blacks-only water fountains, and play in blacks-only parks. When he went to his grandma's house, he had to ride in the back of the bus behind the white people. Still, his mother taught him to read and love books, and his father taught him discipline and lots of hard work.

When he was four years old, Arthur's father was hired to manage a large park in Richmond. The Ashe family moved into a house in the middle of the blacks-only playground. Arthur could not have been happier. His house was beside a tennis court! By the time he was ten years old, he was playing against people twice his age.

Mr. Ashe graduated with the highest grade-point average in his class at Sumner High School, which earned him a scholarship to the University of California at Los Angeles. He was the first African American student to be given a scholarship to the university. At UCLA, Mr. Ashe worked with some of the country's best tennis coaches. He was happy to find out that his tennis hero, Pancho Gonzales, practiced on the same courts as the UCLA players. Mr. Gonzales worked with Mr. Ashe, helping him develop that powerful serve.

In 1968, Mr. Ashe was the only player to win the singles title at both the United States National Tournament and the United States Open Tournament. He was so respected in the tennis world that companies paid him to use his name on their tennis products.

When he was 31, Mr. Ashe dropped to fifth place in the worldwide tennis standings. People began to think that he was too old to play good tennis. Mr. Ashe surprised everyone by winning the World Championship Tennis Tournament in Dallas. He went on to Wimbledon, where he beat Jimmy Conners. Arthur Ashe was number one again!

In 1988, Arthur Ashe found out he had AIDS. He had become infected when he had a blood transfusion during a heart operation. He started the Arthur Ashe Foundation to try to find a cure for AIDS.

"You're not going to believe this," Mr. Ashe told *People* magazine, "but living with AIDS is not the greatest burden I've had in my life. Being black is."

Arthur Ashe died on February 7, 1993, at the age of 49. His achievements continue to encourage people of all ages who are struggling against difficulties.

Mae Jemison (b. 1956)

On September 12, 1992, Mae Jemison blasted off from Cape Canaveral. She was going on an eight-day journey into space. The little girl from the south side of Chicago had made her dreams come true. Dr. Jemison had become the first African American woman to be launched into space.

Mae Jemison was born October 17, 1956, in Decatur, Alabama. She was the youngest of three children. When she was three years old, she moved to Chicago with her family. As a child, young Mae read lots of books about space and dreamed about traveling there. She watched the Gemini and Apollo launchings and the moon walk on television. She was fascinated. "I don't remember the time I said, 'I want to be an astronaut,'" Dr. Jemison said. "It's just always been there."

Ms. Jemison graduated from Morgan Park High School in Chicago when she was just 16. Her favorite subjects were math and science. She earned a scholarship to Stanford University and graduated with a degree in Chemical Engineering. She went on to Cornell University Medical College in New York and became a medical doctor in 1981.

Dr. Jemison wanted to travel and to use her medical skills, so she entered the Peace Corps in 1983. She worked for two and a half years in West Africa. When she returned from Africa, she decided to file

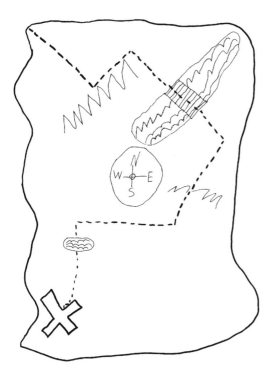

an application with NASA to become an astronaut. She waited and waited. After two years of waiting, she was chosen as one of 15 people to begin training in America's space program. The tragic Challenger rocket accident in 1986 caused many changes in the NASA space program. Ms. Jemison kept on waiting.

It took four more years before she was finally launched into orbit. During her eight days in space, Dr. Jemison traveled 3.3 million miles, studied space motion sickness, and did bone cell research. She also performed experiments with frog eggs. Her 150 tadpoles were the first creatures—other than insects—born in space. Dr. Jemison also studied the effects of zero gravity on animals and people.

Dr. Jemison encourages young African Americans to pursue science careers. However, she doesn't like being considered a role model. She tells young people that they should work hard to make their own dreams come true. They don't have to be an astronaut. That's what Dr. Jemison wanted to do. She made her dreams come to life.

SHORT BIOGRAPHIES

Estevanico Dorantez (?–1539)

Estevanico Dorantez was a black Hispanic explorer who lived in the 1500s. He sailed from Spain to the United States, around the Florida Keys, more than 400 years ago. The expedition he was on traveled for eight years through swamps and rivers to find Mexico City in 1536.

Mr. Dorantez's ship hit some coral reefs, and most of the crew died in the wreck. He and three of the crew were the only survivors. They walked for days. Then, one day, they found a large settlement of Indian pueblos. Mr. Dorantez opened the territory that is now New Mexico and Arizona. In 1539, the Indians killed Estevanico Dorantez.

Elizabeth Freeman (1742–1829)

With the courage of a whole army, Ms. Freeman worked to end slavery in Massachusetts. Elizabeth Freeman grew up in the middle of the 1700s, during the colonial period. She lived in Massachusetts and worked as a slave for Colonel John Ashley. Ms. Freeman was sick and tired of being a slave and felt that since the colonies won their independence, so should she.

After leaving the household of John Ashley and refusing to return, Ms. Freeman went looking for legal help to make sure she would stay free. She found a young lawyer named Theodore Sedgwick and asked him to help her gain freedom. She argued her case before Mr. Sedgwick and convinced him to take it.

In 1781, Ms. Freeman's case was heard by the county court in Great Barrington, Massachusetts. The court agreed that she was a free woman and that there would be no more slavery in Massachusetts. The judge made Colonel Ashley pay Ms. Freeman 30 shillings. A shilling is a gold coin used in the British Commonwealth worth 100 cents in American money. After her victory, Ms. Freeman went to work for the Sedgwick family.

Olaudah Equiano (1745–1801)

Have you ever wanted to know what it would be like to be a slave? Well, Olaudah Equiano wrote a book explaining his life as a slave and how other slaves felt.

Mr. Equiano was born in 1745 in southern Nigeria, a part of Africa. When he was 11, three men picked him up out of his front yard and carried him away. They made him a slave.

Mr. Equiano had many slavemasters. Robert King, a merchant from Philadelphia, was the last person to buy him as a slave. Mr. King gave Mr. Equiano a new name, Gustavus Vassa, and taught him how to buy and sell the things in his store. This allowed Mr.

Equiano to earn money to buy himself out of slavery. Mr. Equiano wrote a book, published in 1789, about his adventures as a slave. It was called *The Interesting Narrative of the Life of Olaudah Equiano, or Gustavus Vassa*.

Norbert Rillieux (1806–1894)

Mr. Rillieux was born in New Orleans, Louisiana, on March 17, 1806. His parents were hard-working people. His dad was a wealthy French engineer, and his mom was a plantation slave woman.

As a young man, Mr. Rillieux was freed and went to Paris to study engineering at L'Ecole Centrale. When he was 24, he became a professor there, specializing in steam engine technology.

Mr. Rillieux designed a "multiple effect vacuum pan" evaporator that improved the quality of sugar and produced it at a lower cost.

Elijah McCoy (1843–1929)

Have you ever wondered where the phrase "the real McCoy" came from? Elijah McCoy was a great inventor. He was famous for inventing a device that would oil machinery automatically. Trains and other machines stopped every single day to be oiled, and it was a waste of money and time. His machine saved both time and money by doing this task automatically. A lot of people tried to copy Elijah McCoy's work, but people kept demanding the original—"the real McCoy."

Edmonia Lewis (1845–1890)

Edmonia Lewis was one of the first African Americans to be recognized as a great artist. Ms. Lewis was a very talented sculptor. People said she could make stones talk because each of her sculptures tells a story. Ms. Lewis sculpted busts of famous people who fought to end slavery. She was also a fighter for freedom, working with the underground railroad. Her father was African American, and her mother was Native American. Ms. Lewis went to Rome, Italy, where she started an arts studio. Edmonia Lewis died when she was 45 years old.

Jan E. Matzeliger (1852–1889)

"Mr. Whitney, could you tell me how your cotton machine works?" Jan Matzeliger asked questions about how different machines worked even when he was young. It's no surprise that he became an inventor.

Mr. Matzeliger left Dutch Guiana for the United States around 1878. He traveled to Lynn, Massachusetts, where he found a job in a shoe company. He watched men lasting (hand-sewing)

leather to the soles of shoes and decided he would try to build a machine that would do the job.

Mr. Matzeliger began experimenting at night in a cheap room he had rented. He used all kinds of odds and ends—even old cigar boxes—to build a model of his machine. Mr. Matzeliger took several years to complete the machine. He received a patent for his "lasting machine" on March 20, 1883. The lasting machine made 150 to 700 shoes a day, instead of only 50. Mr. Matzeliger sold his patent to United Shoe Machinery Company. Because of his invention, Lynn, Massachusetts, became the shoe capital of the world.

Granville T. Woods (1856–1910)

Granville Woods is known as the black Edison. He was born in Columbus, Ohio, in 1856. At the age of ten, he ran away

Granville T. Woods

from school to start work. When he was 16 years old, he moved to Missouri, where he worked as a fireman and a railroad engineer. Then he moved to New York City and studied electrical engineering. Mr. Woods made a telephone transmitter and an electrically heated egg incubator. These are only two of the more than 60 patents credited to him. Many of his patented inventions were sold to such well-known American companies as General Electric, Westinghouse, and Bell Telephone.

Sarah B. Walker

Daniel Hale Williams (1858–1931)

Daniel Hale Williams performed the first heart operation in Chicago's Provident Hospital in 1893. The victim had been stabbed and left to die. Dr. Williams

Daniel Hale Williams

actually sewed up a torn heart without the aid of drugs. When the president of the United States heard about this operation, he made Dr. Williams the chief surgeon of the Freedmen's Hospital in Washington, D.C.

Dr. Williams contributed greatly to the development of surgery and medical careers for black people. Concerned that there was no hospital for blacks in Chicago, Dr. Williams established the Provident Hospital and Training Association in 1891. It provided hospital care for everyone and training for black physicians and nurses.

Sarah B. Walker (1867–1919)
(known as Madame C. J. Walker)

Madame C. J. Walker was born Sarah Breedlove in Delta, Louisiana, on December 23, 1867. Her parents were Owen and Minerva Breedlove. When she was 14 years old, she married, but her husband died young. After he died, she worked as a washerwoman to earn money to educate their daughter. It was hard work.

Soon Madame Walker's hair began falling out. She tried various remedies, but nothing worked. In 1905, she came up with a formula that could be used to help hair growth. Her experiments on herself and her family were successful, so she invented more products to help the skin and hair of African Americans. After she spent a year in preliminary work, she traveled to different places to promote her products. Madame Walker became very wealthy manufacturing and selling her products. In fact, Madame Walker became the first African American woman millionaire.

Charles Henry Turner (1867–1923)

Like most boys, Charles Henry Turner was very interested in nature. He was so fascinated by ants that he would lay on the ground watching them and wondering why they did all that work and how they found their way back to the nest. His teacher told him that if he wanted to know, he had to find out for himself. Charles Turner said, "I will." Later in Dr. Turner's life, he discovered that ants use the light from the sun and other producers of light to find their way home.

Dr. Turner received his doctorate from the University of Chicago in 1907. He began teaching biology and psychology at Sumner High School in 1908. He was a dedicated, outstanding, and inspiring teacher and research scientist.

Dr. Turner looked for answers to his questions during his lifetime. He

became one of the great African American scientists of his century.

Ida B. Wells (1862–1931)

Ida B. Wells was one of the first civil-rights leaders. Ms. Wells had very tough parents. They were born slaves and taught Ms. Wells to be happy that she wasn't a slave. Later in her life, some people were stealing African American lands, and African American men were being hanged for crimes they didn't do. Ms. Wells fought back with words. She also helped start the NAACP.

William Christopher Handy (1873–1958)

William Christopher Handy is known as the "Father of the Blues." When Mr.

W. C. Handy

Handy was in his twenties, he traveled across the United States playing with small bands, trying to earn a few dollars. His first big hit was "Memphis Blues," which started out as an election song for Edward "Boss" Crump, the mayor of Memphis. Crump cheated W. C. Handy by not paying him for his song.

Mr. Handy started the Pace and Handy Music Company. At that time, the blues were becoming popular, and his company became a success. Before this time, blues were thought of as the music of poor people. Even though he had serious eye problems and became blind, he continued to write and publish the music of black America.

Carter G. Woodson (1875–1950)

The first history lesson Carter G. Woodson learned was the history of his own family. He was born in New Canton, Virginia, on December 19, 1875. Even though Mr. Woodson's father could not read or write, he always told all his children, "It is never too late to learn."

Carter Woodson did not attend school until he was 18 years old. He told the principal at Douglass High School, "It is never too late to learn," and he started school. Mr. Woodson learned so fast that he finished high school 18 months later.

Mr. Woodson went to the Philippines to teach some children. He taught them a song called "Come Shake the Lomboy Tree." (A lomboy is a kind of plum.) The children loved the song. After seeing the children so happy, Mr.

Woodson decided to teach them about their own history and heroes. The children enjoyed that too. Then he got an idea to write books about African American history. He became known as the "Father of Black History."

Bessie Coleman (1893–1926)

Bessie Coleman might have said, "Come fly with me aboard my airplane." Ms. Coleman was the first known African American to become an aviator. Ms. Coleman was unable to get her flight training in the United States, so she went across the ocean to a flight training school in France. After she finished her training, she returned home to Chicago as a full-fledged pilot in 1920.

Bessie Smith

Bessie Smith (1894–1937)

Bessie Smith was known as the "Empress of the Blues." Ms. Smith sang in clubs and small southern theaters. She sang about things that gave people "the blues"—things like racism, poverty, and people with broken hearts. Ms. Smith's voice was so beautiful and strong that she didn't need a microphone. Her songs told of the sadness and joy of many African Americans.

In 1923, Ms. Smith went to New York to make her first record. After that, she made several more records. Her song "Down Hearted Blues" sold more than 2 million copies. Many people who heard Bessie Smith sing said that she was one of the greatest blues singers in the history of music.

Marian Anderson

Marian Anderson (b. 1902)

A wonderful opera singer named Marian Anderson was born in Philadelphia in 1902. She says that she always loved music, and she showed an interest in singing ever since she was small.

Little Marian was eight years old when she began singing in the church choir. When she was 22, she was awarded a fellowship that paid for a year of study in Europe. Ms. Anderson sang in Paris, where the people thought she had a wonderful voice.

President Roosevelt's wife wanted Ms. Anderson to sing in the Metropolitan Opera House. At that time, though, the owners wouldn't let her because she was black. So Mrs. Roosevelt had her sing in front of the Lincoln Memorial instead. She eventually did sing at the Metropolitan Opera House and won many honors.

Marian Anderson was the first African American woman ever to be an opera singer.

Ralph Bunche (1904–1971)

Ralph Bunche won the Nobel Peace Prize in 1950. This award was given to him because he worked hard to help countries become more peaceful.

Ralph Bunche was born in Detroit, Michigan, in 1904. He started selling newspapers when he was eight years old because his family was poor. Both his parents had died by the time he was 11 years old, so Ralph went to live with his grandmother.

Mr. Bunche graduated from high school and decided to get a job to help support his grandmother. But she was wise and told him to go to college. Working as a janitor, he saved some money, and later earned a scholarship for college. His neighbors collected money for him to go to Harvard University. Mr. Bunche earned a doctorate in political science and started working for the American government.

During World War II, Dr. Bunche helped the U.S. plan military bases in Africa. He understood the customs and people of Africa and was able to give important information to the military. The United Nations asked Dr. Bunche to help the Arabs and Jews figure out a way to live together peacefully in the Middle East. Both sides thanked him when they were able to reach a temporary peace settlement. Eventually, Dr. Bunche was appointed to one of the most important

positions in the United Nations. He died in 1971. Dr. Bunche was an African American who worked for peace for all races throughout the world.

Gwendolyn Brooks (b. 1917)

Gwendolyn Brooks was the first African American to earn a Pulitzer Prize. Pulitzer Prizes have been given every year since 1917 for outstanding achievements in drama, writing, music, and journalism. In 1950, Ms. Brooks received the prize for her book of poems called *Annie Allen*. Her poems were about the problems of African Americans in big cities. Ms. Brooks was also named the poet lau-

reate for the state of Illinois and was a literature consultant to the Library of Congress.

Gwendolyn Brooks was born in Kansas on June 17, 1917. Her family moved to Chicago when she was a child. When she was 13, she published her first poem in a magazine called *American Childhood*. As a teenager, she published more than 75 poems in the African American newspaper *The Chicago Defender*.

In 1936, Ms. Brooks graduated from Wilson Junior College. Soon after, she took a poetry class at the South Side Community Art Center. Her first job was as a secretary—she hoped the experience would give her information to use in her writing. Ms. Brooks won her first prize in poetry in 1943. The novel she wrote in 1953, *Maud Martha*, is the story of an African American girl growing up in Chicago.

Over the years, Ms. Brooks has helped many young people become writers. She has worked with students at many Chicago schools and taught creative writing at four different colleges. Gwendolyn Brooks is a good poet who has helped a lot of other people become good poets, too. Look for her books at the library.

Althea Gibson (b. 1927)

Althea Gibson set the tone for tennis in the world. She played at Wimbledon even before the famous Arthur Ashe. When she was young, she decided to work hard to be the very best in women's tennis. At the same time, she

was aware that she would be breaking down the barrier in the tennis world for black people.

Althea Gibson grew up in New York City. She became the first African American to win major titles in tennis. She won tournaments such as the French women's singles championship in 1956 and the United States and Wimbledon singles competition in 1957 and 1958. She was also ranked number one in the world among women players in 1957 and 1958. Althea Gibson became an international tennis star and an inspiration to others.

Wilma Rudolph (b. 1940–1994)

Imagine being crippled as a child and having to wear a leg brace to help you

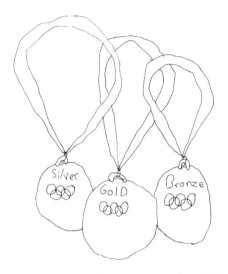

walk. That is what happened to Wilma Rudolph, who got polio and had to wear a leg brace. She worked hard and eventually learned to run without the leg brace. When she ran track in high school, she usually won. Eventually, Ms. Rudolph earned a track scholarship to Tennessee State University and ran on their team. In 1960, she ran in the Rome Olympic Games. She was the first African American woman to win three Olympic medals in track. She was considered the fastest female in the world.

MORE FAMOUS FIRSTS AND HEROES

Here are more people who have accomplished great things. Find out more about many other African Americans at your school or public library.

Phillis Wheatley (1753-1784)
> First African American poet to publish a book.

Paul Cuffee (1759-1817)
> First African American sea captain.

Richard Allen (1760-1831)
> First African American religious leader and bishop.

York (1770-1831)
> Explorer with Lewis and Clark.

James Beckwourth (1798-1867)
> Trapper in the western United States.

Lewis Temple (1800-1854)
> Inventor of a new kind of harpoon.

Ira Aldridge (1807-1867)
> First African American stage actor.

Mary Fields (1832-?)
> African American cowgirl.

Joseph H. Rainey (1832-1887)
> First African American member of the U.S. House of Representatives.

Blanche Kelso Bruce (1841-1898)
> First African American to serve a full term in the U.S. Senate.

Nat Love (1844-1921)
> Famous African American cowboy.

Lewis Latimer (1848-1928)
> Draftsman, inventor.

Henry O. Flipper (1856-1940)
> First African American to graduate from West Point.

Mary Church Terrell (1863–1954)
Women's rights activist.

Matthew A. Henson (1866–1955)
Explorer. First African American to reach the North Pole.

Maggie Lena Walker (1867–1934)
Banker and civil-rights advocate.

Oscar de Priest (1871–1951)
First African American from a northern state to be elected to the U.S. Congress in the twentieth century.

Jack Johnson (1878–1946)
Boxer. First African American heavyweight champion.

A. Philip Randolph (1889–1979)
Organizer of the nation's first trade union for black workers.

Paul Robeson (1898–1976)
Singer, stage actor.

Percy Lavon Julian (1899–1975)
Chemist. Found new treatment for cancer.

Charles "Chief" Anderson (1902–?)
First African American fighter pilot.

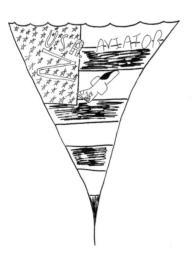

William H. Hastie (1904–1976)
Judge. First African American to be appointed a U.S. federal judge.

Richard Wright (1908–1960)
Author. Wrote *Native Son* and *Black Boy*.

Adam Clayton Powell (1908–1972)
First African American to be elected to the New York City Council; a strong leader for black rights.

Katherin Dunham (b. 1910)
Dancer, choreographer, and anthropologist.

Mahalia Jackson (1911–1972)
World-renowned gospel singer.

Judge Berton Parsons (b. 1911)
Teacher, lawyer, and musician. First African American to be appointed a U.S. federal district judge.

Billie Holiday (1915–1959)
Great jazz singer.

Lena Horne (b. 1917)
Award-winning actress and singer.

Alex Haley (1921–1992)
Author. Pulitzer Prize-winning author of *Roots*.

Constance Baker Motley (b. 1921)
Lawyer. The first African American person and first woman to be elected Manhattan borough president in New York City.

Sammy Davis Jr. (1925–1990)
Dancer, actor, and singer. A leader who opened the door for African Americans in the entertainment field.

Angela D. Ferguson (b. 1925)
Researcher for sickle cell anemia, a hospital builder, and a pediatric doctor.

Coretta Scott King (b. 1927)
> Civil rights activist. Wife of Martin Luther King Jr.

Carl B. Stokes (b. 1927)
> Lawyer. First African American mayor of Cleveland, Ohio, in 1967.

Sidney Poitier (b. 1927)
> In 1963, he received the Academy Award for best actor for his performance in *Lilies of the Field*.

Maya Angelou (b. 1928)
> Author, memoirist. Best known for her book *I Know Why the Caged Bird Sings*.

Toni Morrison (b. 1931)
> Novelist. Toni Morrison's first novel, *Beloved*, won the Pulitzer Prize for Literature in 1988.

Andrew Young (b. 1932)
> Politician. Civil rights leader; congressman from Georgia; U.S. ambassador to the United Nations, 1977–1979; mayor of Atlanta, 1982–1989.

Bill Russell (b. 1934)
> Athlete. First African American to become a head coach in any professional sport.

Barbara Jordan (1936–1996)
> Politician. Former congresswoman from Texas; member, House Judiciary Committee.

Colin Powell (b. 1937)
> First African American chairman of Joint Chiefs of Staff.

Marian Wright Edelman (b. 1939)
> Set up Children's Defense Fund.

Oprah Winfrey

Jesse Jackson (b. 1941)
> Minister and civil rights leader. Ran for president of the U.S. in 1984 and 1988.

Muhammad Ali (b. 1942)
> Boxer. Born Cassius Clay. Heavyweight champion of the world, 1964–1967, 1974–1978.

Guion Stewart Bluford Jr. (b. 1942)
> Astronaut. First African American to travel into space, 1983.

Aretha Franklin (b. 1942)
> Singer, musician. Known as the "Queen of Soul."

Oprah Winfrey (b. 1954)
> Actress, talk show host.

ART, MUSIC, AND DANCE

Colorful art, flowing dance,
Many people taking a chance.
Music from their very souls,
Turning dreams into goals.

In Africa, art, music, and dance are routinely used to celebrate important events in life. Births, deaths, the planting or harvesting of crops, weddings, and hunts all have their own collection of rhythms, dances, and artwork. They are used to spread the news. Even if neighboring villages cannot understand each other's spoken language, they can still tell what is going on through art, music, and dance. When Africans came to the New World, they brought with them this unique tradition of rhythm, movement, and art.

In this section, we will tell you a little bit about African American culture to help you understand the music, dance, and art we enjoy today. We have included directions for making your own Adinkira pins, drums, and rattles. You will also find the names of famous artists, dancers, and musicians you may want to research.

There is enough information here to get you started. If you like this section, remember that there are many books about art, music, and dance waiting for you in your school and public libraries. Do some investigating on your own.

ART

Early African Art

The oldest known African artworks are prehistoric paintings found in a mountain in the Sahara Desert. These were found on rocks, rock shelters, and cave walls, much like Egyptian hieroglyphics and modern graffiti.

African artwork includes sculptures, figures, masks, decorated boxes, and various other objects for ceremonial and everyday use. Many early sculptures were made of wood. Because wood decays, though, few examples of such work are left. Some other artworks were made of bronze, ivory, and terra cotta (a kind of pottery). Few people outside of Africa knew about African art until the 1900s.

When the Africans were brought to the New World, they carried with them a unique art tradition. Their art showed their history, their religious beliefs, and their values.

Kyeke Ko Aware

Adinkira Art

There are many different African crafts. We want to tell you about Adinkira art, which is connected with the African people of central and southern Ghana and the Ivory Coast. The Adinkira are symbols that are used to decorate art and clothing. These symbols can be used to mean different things. We will give you some history of the Adinkira, along with directions for making your own Adinkira pin.

These symbols first originated from a ruler named King Adinkira, who ruled Guyomen. There was a battle, and the king was killed. The Ashanti took his robe with symbols as a trophy and named the cloth after King Adinkira.

In the past, the cloth was worn to funerals as a way of saying good-bye to the dead. The cloth is now worn at any time, not just for grief.

Adinkira Pins

It is said that there are 53 different Adinkira symbols. Look at the pictures on page 56. Find one that you might like to make into a pin. Here's how to make Adinkira symbols.

Materials: You will need newsprint, pin backs or safety pins, art glue, and clay in many colors that can bake in a conventional oven.

1. Choose an Adinkira symbol that you want to make.
2. Get the color of clay you want.
3. Use newsprint paper when working with clay, so your table doesn't turn the color of the clay. Form the clay into balls, coils, or long snakes to form your design. Mold it into the symbol using wild and wonderful colors. On the back of the symbol, be sure to leave an area large enough to attach a pin after it is baked.
4. Bake your clay on aluminum foil at 275 degrees for 20 minutes.
5. Attach a pin back to the back of the Adinkira pin with art glue. Let it dry completely.
6. Wear your pin with pride.

Adinkira pins

Dono Ntoaso

Penpamsie

Aftun Mmireku Denkyem Mmireku

Kerpa

Bi Nka Bi

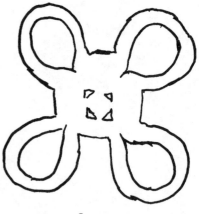

Sunsum

Here are a few Adinkira pins and their names

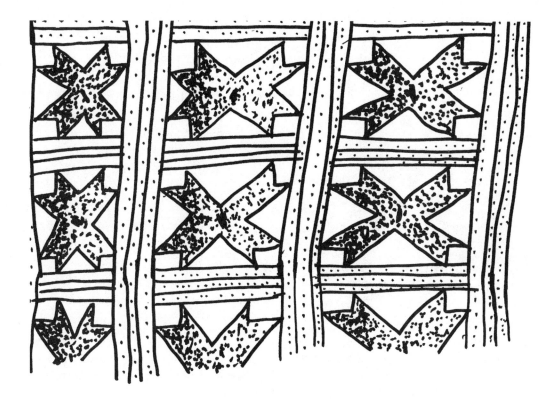

Printing Cloth

You can also print cloth using these same Adinkira symbols, by carving designs into potatoes and then using these potatoes as stamps to print. Follow these directions to do it!

Materials: You will need a potato, liquid soap, tempera paint, a knife, and material or a piece of clothing.

1. Add a little bit of liquid soap to your paint for an easier cleanup.
2. Cut a potato in half width-wise.
3. Carve an Adinkira design or one of your own designs into the potato with a knife.
4. Place the design side of the potato into tempera paint of any color.
5. Stamp the design on a shirt, paper, or whatever you choose.
6. Let it dry completely.

The Ashanti Africans used these designs on clothes to symbolize how they felt. Many African Americans wear these designs on traditional clothes for special celebrations across our country.

Drums

We like the sound of drums because the sound makes us feel weird. You can make lots of sounds with drums.

In Africa, drums were used to communicate over long distances. Different beats, speeds, rhythms, and loudness meant different things to the listener.

This custom was brought to America by slaves. Many people in America play African drums today and create beautiful music.

The drum is a percussion instrument that is played by hitting it. The body of a drum can be shaped like an open cylinder or kettle. The top is covered by a drumhead. The drumheads are made of calfskin or plastic. A cylinder-shaped drum could have two drumheads. A kettle-shaped instrument has only one. The size of the drum determines the pitch. Large drums produce deep, low sounds, and small drums have high-pitched sounds.

African musicians played horns, flutes, lyres, and zithers as well as drums. The drum is one of the oldest musical instruments in the world and had its beginnings in Africa.

We're sure that you will enjoy playing your drum as much as you enjoy making it.

Making a Drum

Materials: To make your own fantastic drum, you will need a coffee can, can opener, duct tape, colored paper, scissors, masking tape, and colorful yarn.

1. Start by removing the top and bottom from your can with the can opener. Be careful not to cut yourself. Pound down any rough edges.

2. Stretch the duct tape over one end of the can. First, place one strip across the center of the can. The second strip should be placed in the other direction to form a cross. Then add more strips that overlap each other, until you cover the top of the can. Each strip of duct tape should be pulled tightly. Put a piece of tape around the edge of the can to cover the ends of the strips.

3. Cover the outside of the can with paper. Fasten the paper to the can with masking tape.

Kent Rucker shows students how to make a drum.

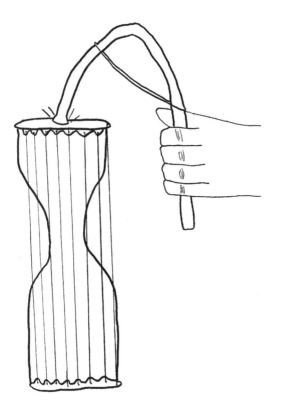

Rattles

Another ancient instrument that is fun to play is the rattle. Some dancers used rattles when they performed, and some musicians used them to accompany drums. Rattles can be made of different materials. We made our rattles using paper, but usually they are made out of gourds. Gourd seeds, such as squash, take four months to grow. The gourds are dried for about nine months. Sometimes the outside layer can be carved to make beautiful designs. Beads can be tied to the outside of the gourd to make music. This type is called a *shakara*. Shakaras are often covered with a hand-beaded "skirt" that adds a different sound when you shake it. Here's how we made our own rattles using paper.

4. Fasten a piece of yarn to one end of the can. Begin turning the can and covering it with yarn.
5. Push the yarn toward the top of the can with your fingers, so the can is completely covered. Use different colors and textures of yarn to make your drum look great. Use a knot to tie the ends of yarn together. Put the ends of the yarn in the part of the can still to be covered. Cover the knot ends as you continue to cover the can.

Making and playing your drum is a wonderful project. Once you have finished, you may want to experiment with the different sounds.

Making rattles

Making a Rattle

Materials: Use balloons, 1½-inch strips of newspaper, art glue or papier-mâché glue, rice or beans, a stick 8 inches long, tape, acrylic paint, and brushes.

1. Blow up the balloon to the size of a grapefruit and tie the end.
2. Insert a paper clip at the mouth of the balloon and tape it to the table to hold it in place. This way, it won't move while you are working on it. Later, you can use the paper clip to hang the balloon up to dry.
3. Dip the 1½-inch strips of newspaper into the papier-mâché glue. Put the strip between your index finger and middle finger and slowly slide your fingers down the strip to remove excess glue. Do this over the bowl of glue so you don't make a mess and make your mother upset.
4. Lay a strip on the balloon. Smooth the paper flat so your rattle will look neat. Repeat until the balloon is covered. This will take about three layers of paper. You might use plain newsprint for the second layer so you can see where you have been. Be sure and smooth out each layer.
5. Hang your balloon up by the paper clip so it can dry. This should take a day or two.
6. After your balloon has dried, remove the paper clip and, without hurting the papier-mâché, poke it into the balloon to pop it. Now pull the balloon out of your rattle.
7. Use a funnel in the hole you took the balloon out of to pour rice or beans into your rattle. As you put your rice or beans into the rattle, listen to the sound. Continue to add the rice or beans until you get the sound you

Authors put papier-mâché on balloons to make their rattles.

Painting the rattles

like. Don't use too many beans or rice kernels, or the rattle will be too heavy, and your stick won't hold it up. Put your stick into the rattle and push in until the stick touches the top of the inside of the rattle. Tape your stick to your rattle so that it doesn't move and the hole is completely covered.

8. Paint your rattle. Cover first with one color. When the paint is dry, decorate the rattle with Adinkira symbols (pgs. 54–56) or other designs to make it beautiful.

9. Now you're ready to make wonderful and exciting music. Just shake the rattle to your own special beat.

African Art in the United States

Because slaves were brought from many different parts of Africa, each with a different language, the Africans in America could not talk to each other. Art is a form of communication that brings people together, no matter what language they speak. The first Africans in America never had a chance to show their African heritage through art because the slave owners knew that this was one of their common means of communication. They feared the slaves would get together, destroy the plantation, and escape, so they discouraged art. In recent years, however, black art has been rediscovered and has become very popular.

The first recorded African American artist was Scipio Morehead in the 1700s in Boston. Even though he was living in America, he painted in the European style. There were more black artists during this time, but a lot of their work was lost. Some black artwork done by slaves was practical, including brass locks, hinges, bureaus and other furniture, rugs, egg baskets, cooking utensils, wooden banisters, and tools. Peter Simmons, born a slave, made beautiful iron gates that still hang today. Certain dolls for white children were made by a slave named Emmaline.

Blacks with talent did artwork to buy their freedom. They were coach makers, sign painters, silversmiths, ship makers, ornament makers, and quilters. An example of this is in Sidney Lanier's home, where there are quilts done by slaves showing the "log cabin" and "fan pattern" designs. Because the works of art done by slaves weren't signed, you may have an authentic piece of slave art in your home and not even know it.

There was a type of art popular among some white Americans that showed blacks as clowns and fools. Images of blacks, like Aunt Jemima, appeared eating watermelons or as entertainers and singers. These characters all had black faces and big pink lips and were used to advertise such products as Czar's Baking Powder and Dixon's Stove Polish.

These images were examples of stereotypes that show blacks as being slow, lazy, dumb, and childish. Some of these stereotypes still exist today. People pass these negative thoughts on to other

Dolls made for white children by a slave named Emmaline

Mural at Mitchell Elementary School in Denver, Colorado

people, when everyone should be left to get to know people for themselves.

There were some black and white artists who showed blacks as they really are. They painted blacks in church, work, and family settings. These artists showed blacks with dignity, class, and style. People in these images posed gracefully, with strength and intelligence. Until recently, though, few black artists earned enough money to support their families and themselves, because themes such as slavery, sharecropping, or ghetto life have not always been sought after by leading art dealers.

In the nineteenth century, African American artists were better documented. Some of them are Robert Duncanson, William Simpson, Edward Bannister, Joshua Johnston, Douglass Bowser, Edmonia Lewis, Henry Tanner, William Harper, and Meta Warwick Fuller. These artists used the styles that were popular in Europe. Later on, blacks started to do more works that reflected their own black heritage instead of the European heritage and history.

Early in the twentieth century, Harlem—an area of New York City— became the center of a tremendous amount of creative art done by black artists. Black culture began to be recognized, accepted, and appreciated by whites. This caused the desegregation of New York theaters and provided an outlet for African Americans to create a variety of art forms. This became known as the Harlem Renaissance.

During the Depression, some black artists were employed by the Works Progress Administration (WPA). They had many jobs, one of which was painting murals. Some of their murals can still be seen across the country, from New York to Los Angeles. In the 1950s and 1960s, art done by black artists searching for black identity consisted of murals depicting street and ghetto life. Another form of wall art called graffiti was started in large cities by youth of every culture. Graffiti began when kids sprayed paint secretly (and usually illegally) on walls of public places, such as subways or the sides of buildings. This kind of art became a competition between neighborhood kids. They painted on walls or over other people's graffiti and tried not to get caught. In New York, graffiti still appears on subway trains, but now it can also be seen in a few art galleries. Some cities even have specific places where graffiti can be painted legally.

Art Museums

If you and your family are traveling, you might want to visit an African American art museum in another part of the country. Some well-known museums are:

Washington, D.C.
- The Museum of African Art
- Anacostia Museum

Chicago, Illinois
- DuSable Museum

New York, New York
- The Museum for African Art
- Studio Museum in Harlem
- Metropolitan Museum of Art
- The New Museum

For more museums, check the resource guide in the back of this book.

You can also look in your Yellow Pages directory for the African American museum nearest you, or call your local art museum for information on African American exhibits.

Black Artists

There are a number of talented black artists. Here are some black artists that you may want to do some further research on:

Benny Andrews (b. 1930)
> A famous folk artist and sculptor. He is also one of the best collage artists in the U.S.

Elizabeth Catlett-Mora (b. 1919)
> A sculptor and printmaker. She has works in more than a dozen museums and galleries.

Barbara Chase-Riboud (b. 1939)
> A famous sculptor who does shows around the world.

Ed Dwight (b. 1930)
> A bronze sculptor in Denver, Colorado. He is gaining nationwide recognition for his work.

MUSIC

The various types of music we are going to tell about all come from our African American heritage. This is just a brief introduction to these forms of music.

Spirituals

Spirituals, the earliest African American music, were brought from Africa. In

little but their belief in God, so they sang about that a lot. They sang songs that would have reached right down into your soul.

The slaves were not permitted to gather together because their owners thought they might make plans to get away. The only reason they could meet was to celebrate their belief in God. One of the songs they sang that came from Africa was "Kumbaya," in which they asked God to "come by here."

African Americans also sang songs about freedom and escape that were disguised as spirituals. There was a ship called *Jesus* that helped slaves get away. When they wanted to tell people to run away, they would sing "Steal Away to Jesus." They also sang "Down by the Riverside" to tell people where to go to

Africa, people had music and special rhythms for everything they did. In America, the slaves didn't have fancy instruments, so they used anything they could find. They used their music as a form of communication—calling out their message and then having others answer them.

For example, while working in a field, someone would start a song, and others would answer, until everyone joined in. The people were very creative and made up the songs on the spot. They sang about things like pain, agony, and death. They also sang about love, justice, and mercy. The slaves had very

escape. Other songs that sent messages were "Get on Board, Little Children" and "The Old Ship of Zion." In this song, the words are, "'Tis the old ship of Zion. It has landed many a thousand. Get on board, get on board." The slaves understood the message, and many escaped. Some spirituals have been printed in church songbooks, but they don't give credit to the slaves. They call them American folk songs or traditional songs. Next time you hear a spiritual, see if you can figure out if they contain any coded messages the slaves were sending to their friends.

Development of Modern African American Music

Singers in later years changed the rhythm and style of these songs and developed gospel, blues, jazz, rock 'n' roll, and country music. Dr. Thomas Dorsey wrote "Precious Lord, Take My Hand" when his wife and only child died. This is considered one of the first gospel songs. Now, you almost never have a funeral in the black community without that song. It has become almost a theme song for many funerals today.

Gospel music is loved by nearly everyone. People like the emotional part that speaks to their souls. The songs talk about the feeling between you and your God. The songs are very free-form, with people clapping their hands and tapping their feet to the music. You sing gospel music the way you feel it. Many black musicians have not been formally trained, so they play by ear.

The early rural church in the South only had a few instruments—often only a tambourine. The voice was the best instrument. Sometimes singers competed with each other to see who could sing highest or lowest. The congregation also sang about how they felt. Everyone sang together in rhythm and made beautiful music.

Ragtime music is happy and full of bounce. It has a melody that consists of quick abbreviated notes. It was called "stepping music" because a person could step to the beat. It was first heard at the turn of the century, but it became even more popular in the 1970s. Only a handful of people wrote ragtime songs, or "rags," as they were called. A good place to hear ragtime is in the movie *The Sting*.

Jazz is a combination of ragtime and blues. It can be either bright and cheery or low and sad—or all of those in the same song. Jazz can come to you from out of nowhere. It is unpredictable, which means you don't know what to expect next. Jazz is very complicated because it uses more rhythms, instruments, and vocals. Jazz started with only instruments. Then words were put to the music. There is always a basic melody, and then the players start adding their own ideas to expand on the original music.

The blues is another variation of the spiritual. Most of its themes are about love and the good and bad feelings a person has. It's sung for the public, so it doesn't have religious words. Blues songs are sometimes really slow-paced and use a lot of guitar chords. The words to the songs are the most important part. The singer can change them as he or she goes along. The people in a blues audience feel the emotions of the performer. They can respond by saying, "Yeah," "Tell it like it is," or "That's right."

Rap, the newest African American music, started back in Africa. In African tribes, "men of words," or rappers, told stories and shared their wisdom with their audiences. Rap is a verbal communication using lyrics that rhyme to express a story. The chants and background music are sometimes directly related to African chants and rhythms. Some of the dances used with rap come from dances performed by warriors. They are inspired by the beat of the drum, just like the music played by Zulu warriors when marching off to war.

Rap is everywhere. It's so popular that young people can recite rhyming lyrics without preparation at speeds of up to 250 words per minute. It has influenced the way people dress, speak, dance, and behave.

Types of African drums

There are different kinds of rap styles. Like other forms of music, rap has its bad points. Some of the rappers sing about crime, drugs, and sex. This style is known as "ghetto" or "hard-core" rap. Recordings of this kind of rap have warnings on the labels telling about the bad stuff in it.

Rap has become a new form of communication between people. It expresses the rapper's thoughts and relationship with society. Many times people can relate to the lyrics and find comfort or satisfaction by listening to rap music.

All the music we have written about comes from the slave experience. Even through the hard times, African Americans gave much to the arts. A lot of the styles and rhythms that we find so exciting and new today began in Africa and were brought to us by the first Africans who arrived in America. All American music is indebted to these people for giving us a feeling that can't be defined. It is called "soul."

African American Performers

If you want to learn more about African American musical performers, you might do more research on the following people:

Louis Armstrong (1900–1971)
   Sang and played the trumpet.
James Brown (b. 1934)
   "Godfather of Soul." Rock 'n' roll singer and dancer.

Duke Ellington (1899–1974)
Band leader.

Ferdinand "Jelly Roll" Morton
(1890–1941)
Piano player. Claimed that he had invented jazz in 1902.

Diana Ross (b. 1944)
Singer. Formed the group called the Supremes.

Scott Joplin (1868–1917)
Famous composer of ragtime.

Jimi Hendrix (1942–1970)
A rock singer and famous guitar player. Considered by some to be the greatest guitarist of all time.

Richard "Little Richard" Penniman
(b. 1932)
Popular rock 'n' roll singer who inspired Elvis Presley, the Beatles, the Rolling Stones, and Prince, among others.

Leontyne Price (b. 1927)
First African American to sing opera on television.

Charley Pride (b. 1938)
First black to enjoy a successful country-western music career.

DANCE

African dance has influenced many of the American dances we perform today. From the cakewalk to break dancing, we can trace the movements back to their roots in Africa. Most dancing was done in a single line, in two parallel lines, or in a circle. The dancers listened to the sounds of the drums and moved to the beat. Since each drum played a different beat, some dancers would have different parts of their bodies following different rhythms.

In America, slave owners often wouldn't let slaves dance. So they would go into the woods at night to do African dances without being seen. One of the dances they did was the *capoeira* (COP-o-ye-da), a dance that looks like karate. It has sharp kicking motions. It is actually a dance the slaves used to practice to help protect themselves. It is still performed every day in Brazil.

Some people call tap-dancing an American folk dance, but it really came from African tribes who pounded the earth with their bare feet. They used their heels to tap out rhythms on sun-

baked clay. On the way to America, slaves were forced to dance aboard the ships to exercise, because even then, people knew you needed to exercise to stay healthy and strong. The Africans used the foot-stomping rhythms and mixed them with the dances of the sailors. In the New World, they did the same thing on the floors of their huts or the boards of their dancing floors.

Later, metal "taps" were put on the heels and toes of the dancer's shoes to make noise. Tap-dancers now use many different steps, such as the shuffle, buffalo, ball-change, soft-shoe, and continental. These steps are combined with clapping, slides, and props to create unforgettable sights, sounds, and rhythms. Bill "Bojangles" Robinson, Sammy Davis Jr., and brothers Gregory and Maurice Hines have all contributed to the American style of tap-dancing that is popular today.

The slaves did many dances that included placing buckets or glasses of water on their heads to show balancing skills. In the cakewalk, couples created steps to go along with the quick, short beats of the music. They had to dance along a straight path without letting the water spill. After the dancing was over, the couple that did the best job would be given a cake. The cakewalk is still used all across America as a fun contest at church or community parties, but usually without the glass of water.

Sometimes people made up dances by trying to move like a certain animal. The camel walk was a dance in which people tried to imitate the camel's walk. It was done by bending one knee in a jerky motion while putting the opposite heel down. A dancer who is good at it will look just like a camel walking. The dancers also did dances called the turkey trot, fish tail, and mosquito dance. In the 1960s, young people did "the monkey."

The black bottom was a dance that was introduced in 1924. It later became as popular as the Charleston. It was based on a black challenge dance in which dancers tried to outdo each other. During part of the dance, the dancers slapped their backsides while hopping forward and backward.

In recent times, another challenge dance was born—break dancing. This type of dance started in the inner cities, where some kids used it as a form of competition that didn't involve fighting or hurting each other. The dancers move and spin, bending their bodies in different ways. Break dancing is usually done by young boys and men. The faster the dancer goes and the more different ways he moves, the better people enjoy his dance. Break dancing is very difficult, and it's easy to get hurt doing it, but it's exciting and fun to watch.

A nice thing about dance is that it is always changing to go along with new music that becomes popular. African American dance styles influenced rock 'n' roll music in its very early years. Chubby Checker introduced a Haitian dance, called the *coye*, when he came out with his now-famous song, "The

Twist." Rock 'n' roll is a melting pot of African American gospel, rhythm and blues, as well as country and western. Black America had people singing and dancing to the twist, hully gully, mashed potato, watusi, and the swim.

From Africa to the present day, black people have used dance as a way to express their feelings and experiences. Even now, on many of the dance floors in America, you see traditional movements from Africa.

Remember, there are many fun ways to learn more about dance. You might find out if your community has a cultural center that teaches African American dances. You could also attend an African American celebration to watch or take part in dancing. The local library will also have books on African American dance.

African American Dancers

If you would like to learn more about African American dancers, try looking up these people in your school or local library:

Alvin Ailey (b. 1931)
Formed the Alvin Ailey American Dance Theatre.
Talley Beatty (b. 1923)
Best known for his work in musical comedies and the minstrel ballet.

Katherine Dunham (b. 1910)

Studied dances from Jamaica and served as a dancer and choreographer in motion pictures and musicals.

Gregory Hines (b. 1946)

Known for his dancing and acting abilities.

Judith Jamison (b. 1943)

Co-director of the Alvin Ailey American Dance Theatre.

Arthur Mitchell (b. 1934)

First black principal dancer for the New York City Ballet.

Pearl Primus (b. 1919)

Performed a collection of dances based on African movements.

Bill Robinson (1878–1949)

Better known as "Bojangles." Considered the most famous of all black tap-dancers.

As you leave this section of our book, remember the creative energy and the talent for improvisation that African Americans have added to America's art, music, and dance. Their style has been copied by others and has become truly a part of our American heritage. Music, dance, and art are wonderful gifts that African Americans have given and continue to give to our country. Our lives are touched by this culture every day.

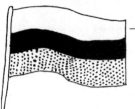

FUN, FOOD, AND CELEBRATIONS

As you turn the pages, you will see
Many good things and new recipes.
Celebrations are such fun,
With food and games for everyone.

CELEBRATIONS

Celebrations can happen any-where, any place, at any time, and for any reason. We want to share some African American celebrations, both national and regional, which bring African Americans together. Celebrations you will learn about are Juneteenth, Junkanoo, Kwanzaa, and Harambee. Our nation also has holidays to honor Martin Luther King Jr. and Malcolm X and a month to celebrate black history.

We will share recipes and ideas for social gatherings, where people get together and have fun. At parties like this, people eat delicious food, dance, and listen to cool music. Taking part in an African American celebration helps you learn history and culture in a happy, exciting way.

Freedom Celebrations

African Americans throughout the United States have various kinds of Freedom Day celebrations to recognize the emancipa-tion (freedom) of their ancestors from slavery. These freedom celebrations are held on different dates in different areas of the country, depending on when slaves were freed in that region. Slaves were freed at different times because news of the emancipation traveled slowly. Things like fax machines, television, and tele-phones were not yet invented. Also, some of the former slave owners had to be forced by the Union Army to follow the Emancipation Proclamation.

January 1 is one of the most common dates for African Americans to celebrate freedom, because the foreign slave trade was officially forbidden in America on that date in 1801. Also, President Lincoln declared that the Emancipation Proclamation was to be followed as of January 1, 1863.

Emancipation Day is called "Juneteenth" in Kansas, Texas, and parts of the Southwest. It is celebrated on June 19. On this day in 1865, a Union general arrived in Galveston, Texas, and read a government order freeing all the slaves in East Texas.

African Americans in Washington, D.C., have two Freedom Day celebrations. They celebrate Juneteenth on the Saturday closest to June 19, and they also celebrate it on April 16, the day slavery was abolished in the District of Columbia in 1862.

Freedom Day is also celebrated at many other times, in May, August, February, and October. For example, Jerry Rescue Day is a freedom celebration held in Syracuse, New York, which began on October 1, 1851. On this date a group of white citizens in Syracuse freed a slave named Jerry and sent him to live in freedom in Canada. The exact historical events surrounding some of the dates are not known. The people who are celebrating simply know that their ancestors were freed on that date.

When people celebrate Juneteenth or Emancipation Day, there are parades, speeches, carnivals, prayers, sermons, readings of the Emancipation Proclamation, singing, bazaars, and picnics. The Washington, D.C., Juneteenth celebration is sponsored by the Anacostia Museum at the Smithsonian Institution. It even includes a play on Harriet Tubman and the underground railroad. No matter where or when it is celebrated, Juneteenth is a holiday that brings back the memories of slavery, celebrates freedom, and promotes the traditions of Africa.

If you want to find out about a Freedom Day celebration, you can call the local library or an African American newspaper. Attend one. You will have fun!

Junkanoo

During the time of slavery, a tradition known as Junkanoo was started by the Bahamians (the native people of the Bahamas). Black slaves were brought from the Bahamas to present-day Miami to work on a railroad. This was hard labor in the swamplands of Florida.

At Christmastime, the black slaves in this area were kept very busy doing work to prepare for the slave masters' Christmas celebration. It wasn't until the day after Christmas that the black slaves were allowed to begin their own Christmas celebration. This celebration from the day after Christmas until New Year's Day was called Junkanoo. It is a very special holiday that must be prepared for months in advance.

The highlight of Junkanoo is a competition between various bands. The members of the bands play whistles and drums and wear fancy, colorful costumes. The competition between bands is fierce, and often the different bands will go off to a secret place six months before Junkanoo to work on their costumes and music. On Junkanoo, the bands parade and prizes are awarded to the most colorful and elaborate. The Junkanoo parades are similar to the Mardi Gras parades in New Orleans.

Today, Junkanoo is still celebrated in the Bahamas. In Jamaica, it is called O'Mass, and in Trinidad, it is called Carnival. It is also celebrated in Miami, Florida.

Kwanzaa

Have you ever been to a Kwanzaa celebration? Kwanzaa is a unique African American holiday that comes from African tradition. *Kwanzaa* is a word for the first fruits of the harvest, and the name is actually taken from the East African word *Kiswahila*. Kwanzaa is celebrated in the wintertime, during the week of December 26 through January 1.

It has traditions similar to those of Thanksgiving, Christmas, and Hanukkah— all rolled into one.

During this celebration time, some people decorate their houses in black, green, and red and fly the African flag. In the flag, black stands for the color of their skin, green is for the land, and red is for the blood they have shed. Some people may think that Kwanzaa is a religious holiday, but it really is not. It is a cultural celebration.

In the spirit of Kwanzaa, women wear a *lappa* or *bubba,* which is a name for an African dress. Men and boys wear *dashikis* (dah-SHEE-kees) or *kanzus* (can-SHOOS). They are traditional dresses for African men. They wear *kofis* (KOH-fees) on their heads and beads around their necks.

Kwanzaa is based on seven principles. They are self-determination, unity,

Kwanzaa

collective work and responsibility, cooperative economics, purpose, creativity, and faith.

On the night before the last day of Kwanzaa, children give presents to their parents which remind them of Africa or their African American ancestors. Children earn their own presents by keeping their promises from the past year. They do not eat from sunrise to sunset, but in the evening, they all gather around and feast. To us, and to many others, Kwanzaa is a very strong African American tradition.

Honoring Black History

In cities across our nation, there are different and exciting things going on in February. This is because February is Black History month. Many museums and centers across the United States plan events and celebrations that highlight African American heritage. For example, the Denver Museum of Natural History sponsors an African American cultural program. People are allowed to play African musical instruments and touch some everyday objects that are exhibited. There are art demonstrations, African dancers, and drummers, as well.

Go to your local library or your African American history museum for more information about the events in your area.

Honoring Martin Luther King Jr.

Martin Luther King Jr. played a great part in history. We recognize him as an outstanding man who helped others to realize racism and prejudice are wrong. When Dr. King was little, he wondered why he couldn't sit by his white friends on the bus or couldn't drink out of the same drinking fountain. As he grew older, he tried to make people understand that black and white are the same. He also said, "Judge people by the content of their character and not the color of their skin." This means a lot to us because we believe that you should not judge people by the color of their skin.

After Martin Luther King's death, the third Monday in January was set aside for people to celebrate his hard work and dedication with speeches and parades. We hope that people will remember him every day by respecting others and not judging them by the color of their skin.

Honoring Malcolm X

Some communities across the United States set aside a special day to remember Malcolm X. One of these is his hometown of Omaha, Nebraska. Every year on March 19, Malcolm X's birthday, there are celebrations and parades down Main Street in Omaha. Malcolm X was an African American leader who spoke out angrily against segregation and unfair treatment of black people in the 1950s and 1960s. Although Malcom X was assassinated in 1965, his ideas still have great influence over the African American community.

Harambee

In October 1974, citizens of the African American community in Dallas, Texas, decided to organize a celebration called Harambee. The celebration was designed to be a safer alternative to Halloween. The people also felt that Halloween didn't really have much significance for African Americans.

Harambee is a celebration of the African American culture. *Harambee* is a Swahili (East African language) word meaning "unity" or "let's pull together." The Harambee celebration is held at the

Martin Luther King Memorial Center in Dallas every October. At the celebration, there are African American art exhibits, films, dance and theater shows, and authentic African foods.

In 1974, the first year that the Harambee celebration was held, more than 3,000 people of all ages, backgrounds, and races participated. The celebration has grown every year! Harambee has really lived up to its name and has pulled the Dallas community together. It is a positive, safe celebration that allows people to experience African American culture.

Traditional Gatherings of Friends and Family

Many years ago, after a hard day's work in the field, the slaves would join friends in singing spirituals and toe tapping. Now, as it was back then, it is still fun to spend the weekend getting together and going to church after working all week. Saturday night fish fries are still popular today because people can talk, share, and feast.

A big tradition all across America is the family reunion. Many African American families have reunions in which family members from different states come to be together. Family reunions remind us of Sunday dinner, when we go to our grandma's house, and she fixes soul food like you will find described next. We eat many delicious foods like fried chicken, greens, cornbread, black-eyed peas, ribs, and catfish.

Funerals also bring family members together. People eat tasty food while

sharing good memories of the person who has died.

These family gatherings are traditional to all cultures in America, but one of the secret ingredients of an African American celebration is traditional food.

FOODS

At first, African American foods were prepared in many ways. Meat was smoked in a smokehouse to make sure it wouldn't spoil. (Remember, there were no freezers or refrigerators at that time.) Drinks were made from the juices of fruits. Meats were barbecued, roasted, boiled, or made into stews. Vegetables were boiled or fried. Feathered wildlife was prepared by frying, baking, roasting, making broths, or simmering to form gravies. In the rivers and streams, there were a lot of fish and other water life that could be eaten. Meals were cooked in open fires using black kettles or were barbecued in open pits. The people who cooked just knew how to do it. They didn't need to follow a recipe.

The slaves were often forced to eat the scraps that the slave masters did not want. They turned these scraps into delicious stick-to-the-rib dishes. Some of these foods are black-eyed peas, cornbread, bread pudding, greens, sweet potato pie, and chitlins.

From this tradition came many mouth-watering African American foods. You will learn about some of the ways African Americans grew, cooked, and seasoned their food and their beliefs about what certain foods could do.

Cornbread and sweet potato pie

You might like to cook some of these African American foods. Come on, treat yourself and try to make some of these wonderful new dishes!

Herbs

Black people brought herbs from Africa to America. Herbs are plants that grow in the ground or on a tree. They can be dried and stored to season foods later and make them taste better. They also make foods smell better. Some examples of herbs are dill, parsley, and sage. Slaves planted the herbs in a little garden on a patch of land by the slave house.

African Americans also used the herbs to impress their slave masters, so they could go into the kitchen and cook for their family. If they were asked to cook for the family, they might be treated better.

In the earlier days when slaves were delivering babies, they would use herbs to stop infection and help the mother. Herbs can also be used to do many other things. For example, you can drink the sassafras herb to help clean out your blood.

Mint is a type of herb that we had in our workshop, and we used three different kinds: peppermint, spearmint, and catnip. We tasted peppermint, and it was our favorite. Spearmint is an awfully good mint too. Catnip was okay. Some liked it. However, some didn't like drinking the catnip tea because cats like to play in catnip plants. They didn't want to drink something cats played in.

Making tea the old-fashioned way is fun. When we tasted the mint tea, we couldn't believe how wonderful it was. It is fun to have on a hot summer day when you need refreshment! Just add ice and you have a nice cool drink and good breath too! We all know how important this is to us older kids.

Fresh Mint Tea

¼   pound fresh mint leaves
2   quarts cold water

Place the mint in cheesecloth and tie with a string. Then place the package into water in a large pan and cover. Bring to a boil, turn the fire low, and let sit for 30 minutes. Sweeten to taste and serve hot. You may also serve this tea over ice with a garnish of fresh mint and lemon.

Sassafras Tea

3   ounces sassafras bark
3   quarts cold water

Place the sassafras leaves in cheesecloth and tie with a string. Place the leaves in a large container, add cold water, and bring to a boil. Then cover and simmer for 20 to 30 minutes, depending on how strong you like it. Add sugar to taste and serve hot or over ice. Many older people prefer to drink their tea hot.

Biscuits

Here is an interesting "biscuit" story about Mary McLeod Bethune, the founder of the National Council of Negro Women. Once when she was on a train trip, they put her in a place for blacks only. The conductor said, "Auntie, do you make good biscuits?" This made her very angry because, out of respect, she should have been called "Miss" or "Mrs.," not "Auntie." She said, "I am an adviser to the president. I am an organizer and founder of the National Council

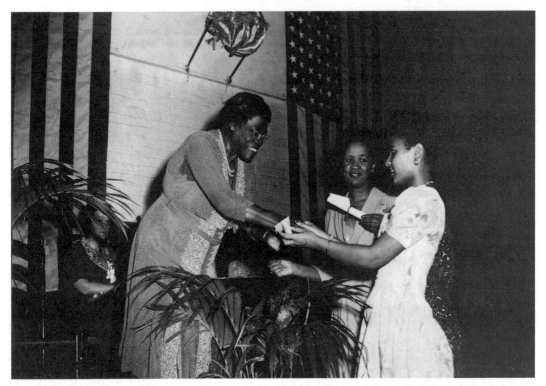

Mary McLeod Bethune giving out diplomas. She founded the National Council of Negro Women and Bethune-Cookman College.

of Negro Women. I am a leader among women! And . . . I make good biscuits!"

We used the following recipe:

Down-Home Biscuits

> 2 cups all-purpose flour
> 1 tablespoon baking powder
> 1 teaspoon salt
> ⅓ cup shortening or cooking oil
> ¾ cup milk

Combine flour, baking powder, and salt in a large bowl. Cut shortening into flour mixture until it forms coarse crumbs. Add milk. Mix with fork until particles cling together. Form dough into a ball and transfer to lightly floured bread board. Knead gently 8 to 10 times. Roll dough out with rolling pin until about ½-inch thick. Cut with 2-inch round cutter or cut into 2-inch squares. Place on baking sheet. Bake at 400 degrees for about 15 minutes.

To make shortcake, add 1 cup sugar. Then prepare the filling and topping. Wash and prepare 2 pints of strawberries. Top with milk, cream, or whipped cream. (Heritage Recipe from *The Black Family Reunion Cookbook* by the National Council of Negro Women.)

Cornmeal

Cornmeal is an important part of the African American diet. There are many ways to use cornmeal. You can fry it to make fritters, or you can bake it to make cornbread. You can even make corn sticks and corn muffins using cornmeal.

Our cornbread was great. It was golden yellow and tasted sweet and delicious. Cornbread is a fast and easy dish to make when you're in a hurry. It is fun to make, tastes great with greens, and is easy for little brothers and sisters to cook.

Cornbread

   1½ cups cornmeal
   ¾ cup flour
   2½ teaspoons baking powder
   ½ teaspoon salt
   1¼ cups buttermilk
   2 eggs
   2 tablespoons oil

Grease a 9-inch pan with oil. Mix all ingredients in a bowl. Pour mixture into the pan and bake in the oven at 425 degrees for 18 minutes.

Corn Pone

   1 cup flour
   1 cup yellow cornmeal
   ½ teaspoon salt
   1 egg
   1 cup milk (or use water)
   2 teaspoons baking powder

Heat skillet, add 1½ tablespoons cooking oil until hot enough that a drop of batter bubbles immediately. Mix flour, cornmeal, salt, egg, and milk or water until smooth with no lumps. Place a spoonful in 4 or 5 places in a hot skillet.

corn pone

Let brown, then turn over like a pancake and brown on the other side. Serve with butter and honey.

Black-Eyed Peas

Black-eyed peas came from Africa. They are a healthy food that people eat to become strong. The black-eyed pea is very tasty and has to be grown in a hot climate. Today they grow in the Deep South. Some African American people believe that if you eat black-eyed peas on New Year's Day, you will have good luck for the new year. We are going to try this next year! It will be fun.

Mom's Black-Eyed Peas

   1 pound black-eyed peas
   4 cups water
   1 medium onion
   ½ teaspoon salt
   ¼ teaspoon pepper
   1 cup cubed ham (optional substitutes: 2 polish sausages, 2 hot sausage links, or bacon)
   ¼ teaspoon dried red pepper (optional)

Pick and wash black-eyed peas. Place in slow cooker or, if you wish to cook them on the top of the stove, a large dutch oven. Combine with salt, pepper, onion, water, and ham or other meat. You can add crushed red pepper if you like spicy food. Simmer on the top of the stove or turn slow cooker to high and allow peas to cook 3 to 4 hours. Serves 6 to 8.

Greens

Does your mom make you eat spinach? In our workshop, we ate greens. Boy, were they good! Greens are vegetable leaves and are very tasty. The basic greens are collards, mustard greens, and turnip greens. There are so many different kinds you can't count them all! In some states such as Kansas, you can pick wild greens such as dandelions, poke salad, and wild lettuce.

Hundreds of years ago when people were slaves, they planted greens on a little piece of land their owners gave them. Some slaves cooked greens in an iron pot. If you were making a "mess of greens," you were cooking a lot of leaves, water, and meat in a big black pot or any kind of pot.

The really great part of cooking greens is the liquid called "pot likker." This is the juice from the vegetables, meat, and leaves when they are cooked. We think it is the best part of all! It is healthy for you if you drain the fat off the meat before adding it to the greens. The flavors are mixed together and really taste good. You can drink it, pour it on top of cornbread, or save it and put it in

the freezer to season the greens the next time you cook some. Here's our recipe for greens.

Home Greens

- 2 bunches turnip greens
- 2 bunches mustard greens
- ½ pound salt pork
- ½ pound of bacon (sliced or cubed)
- ½ teaspoon salt
- ½ teaspoon pepper
- 2 dried red peppers
- ½ medium onion chopped

Place greens in cold water with one teaspoon of salt. Let set for about 10 minutes. Wash greens. Put in plain cold water, picking out any pieces that are bruised or broken. Break off all very large stems. Make sure you wash greens thoroughly, so they are cleansed of any sand or soil. In a large pan, fry meat until browned. Drain off fat if you prefer a healthier meal. Add greens, water, and seasoning. Cover and cook for 1½ hours on low heat, or until greens are tender. Use the leftover juice with greens and cornbread.

Peanuts

On a cold winter night in the Ozark mountains, George Washington Carver, then a tiny baby, was traded for a racehorse worth $300. We think he was a real bargain. Dr. George Washington Carver is the king of the peanut, "The Peanut Wizard." Dr. Carver discovered hundreds of products that could be made from the peanut. He used the peanut to make face powder, printer's ink, and soap, to name just a few. He was a wonderful scientist, and he experimented with many things.

We made many foods from peanuts, including peanut butter, peanut butter balls, peanut butter banana sandwiches, and vegetable peanut butter sandwiches. They were all delicious!

We think you should know something about peanuts before you cook with them. Peanuts grow well in Georgia, Alabama, North Carolina, Texas, and Virginia. They grow underground like a potato. You can eat peanuts many different ways. Peanuts have different names, like goobers, goober peas, ground peas, and pindas. We met a special teacher who does shows on the goober, which is an African name for the peanut. People call this teacher "Mrs. Goober," and you can read about her in the Real People section. Mrs. Goober helped us make these next foods.

Peanut Butter

      2 cups peanuts
   1½ tablespoons sunflower or
          peanut oil

Use a blender or food processor to grind the peanuts. Use a smaller blade if you want finer-ground peanuts. Use bowls to catch the peanuts as they are ground.

Place ¼ cup peanuts and 1 tablespoon oil in blender or grinder. Blend at high speed for 10 to 15 seconds. Slow motor and continue to grind for about 45 more seconds. Use a spatula to remove from blender. If peanut butter is too dry, add more oil. Spread on crackers and serve immediately. Store leftover peanut butter in an airtight jar in the refrigerator.

Peanut Butter Banana Sandwich

      1 teaspoon orange juice
      2 tablespoons peanut butter
      2 sliced bananas
      4 slices brown or grain bread

Add juice to peanut butter and mix until thinned. Spread thinned peanut butter on the bread. Top with banana slices. Cut in halves or quarters and serve.

Vegetable Peanut Butter Sandwich

      1 tablespoon mayonnaise
      2 tablespoons grated carrots
      2 large crisp lettuce leaves
      3 tablespoons peanut butter
      1 tablespoon diced olives
      1 tablespoon diced green peppers
      4 slices bread (white or wheat)

Mix mayonnaise, carrots, olives, and peppers together with peanut butter. Spread on bread, top with lettuce leaf. Cut in ½ or ¼ pieces. Serve immediately.

Other additions for good healthy peanut butter sandwiches are:
      toasted pumpkin seeds
      sunflower seeds
      pickles (sweet or dill)
      cream cheese
      raisins
      cucumbers

Bread Pudding

In the olden days, people could not afford to throw anything away. If they had a lot of leftover old bread (the bread that was made with flour, not cornmeal), they would crumble and save it. The whole message behind bread pudding is that people could not afford to waste or throw away food, so they recycled it. With bread pudding, they used the stale bread to make a delicious dessert. Here's how we did it:

      4 cups dried bread crumbs
      2 eggs beaten
      2 cups milk
   ½ cup sugar

½ teaspoon vanilla
⅛ teaspoon cinnamon
⅛ teaspoon nutmeg
2 tablespoons butter
1½ cups raisins

Mix all the above ingredients. Place in 350 degree oven. Bake for 45 minutes, or until the center is firm to the touch. Can be served hot or cold.

Sweet Potato Pie

We sure liked eating sweet potato pie. A lot of people have pumpkin pie for Thanksgiving, but you can have sweet potato pie instead. This pie is made of yams or sweet potatoes and is really popular in the South. It's delicious! This is what you need:

2 cups cooked mashed sweet potatoes
1⅓ cups sugar (brown or white)
1 teaspoon vanilla extract
1 teaspoon lemon extract
1 teaspoon cinnamon
½ teaspoon nutmeg
3 eggs
½ cup milk or half-and-half
¾ stick of butter

Peel and cube sweet potatoes. Mash potatoes with all the above ingredients. Beat with mixer on medium speed until smooth (or you can mix it by hand until your arm gets tired). Place in pie shell. Bake at 350 degrees for about an hour, or until firm when touched in the middle.

Catfish

Catfish can be cooked different ways—fried, barbecued, baked, or any other way you can think of. When we have cookouts, a lot of people come over. We have barbecued catfish. Fish fries are used as a special time for family and friends to get together. It was fun making this recipe. Our catfish had a spicy, delicious flavor. Ask your mom or dad to help you fry catfish for the family dinner. You need to be careful because this recipe is fried in hot oil.

Fried Catfish Strips

1 catfish fillet
¾ cup cornmeal
½ teaspoon salt
½ teaspoon pepper
1 cup cooking oil

Take the fish fillets and cut into bite-size pieces or little strips. Mix cornmeal, salt, and pepper together. You can season it the way you want by adding some other spices to this mixture. Heat oil to 350 degrees in an electric skillet. Cook on one side until it is golden brown. Turn it over and cook until the

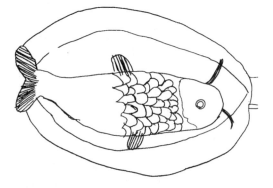

other side is brown, too. Lay the fish on a paper towel to soak up the extra oil.

"Soul" Ice Cream

Many people enjoy eating ice cream in the summer. It's more fun in the summer if you have an old fashioned ice cream freezer and you take it outside, make your own ice cream, and cool off. You turn the handle until the ice cream is frozen. You can also take turns with your friends and family. When the ice cream is hard, take the dasher (this is the beater) out. It's great fun to lick. This is our way to make ice cream. Some people use electric freezers. The ice cream tastes just as good, but it's not as much fun to make. You will need:

    1 cup heavy cream
    1 cup light cream
    ½ cup sugar
    ¾ teaspoon vanilla (optional, can be lemon, nuts, fruit, or other flavors)
    Pinch of salt

    Makes 2 quarts

Using a wooden or plastic spoon, stir contents until sugar dissolves. Place this mixture in an ice cream container. Insert dasher. Place the lid on, and be sure it is snapped or screwed firmly in place. Lock support arm firmly in place. Plug in, if freezer is electric. Have ice and salt ready. Layer ice-salt-ice-salt around the container. As the salt melts the ice, continue to replace it. Freezing time is 20 to 50 minutes. Use your plas-

tic or rubber spatula when stirring in your container, so you do not damage interior or dasher. When the ice cream reaches the consistency you like, remove dasher and serve immediately, or store in the freezer until ready to serve.

Emancipation Proclamation Snackin' Cake

Our special African American cook gave us this wonderful recipe for an easy cake. This cake is called a snackin' cake because you can fix it fast, anytime you want, and eat it as a snack.

A cook demonstrates how to make Emancipation Proclamation Snackin' Cake.

½ cup butter
1 cup sugar
2 eggs
⅔ cup milk
2½ cups flour (sifted)
3 teaspoons baking powder
¼ teaspoon salt
1 teaspoon vanilla extract

Cream butter, add sugar gradually, blend well. Beat eggs well and add to butter and sugar mixture. Mix sifted flour, salt, and baking powder. Add milk a little at a time. Finally, add vanilla. Use two 9" x 12" buttered cake pans. Bake for 30 minutes at 375 degrees.

We hope you try some of these recipes and celebrations. We found them all very exciting. Remember to look around your community for the celebrations they have. This is such a fun and delicious way to learn about the African American heritage.

STORIES, LANGUAGE, AND LITERATURE

As you read these stories,
You will find
Laughter, sadness, hope,
And fun of every kind.

STORIES

When Africans were brought to America as slaves, almost everything was taken away from them. But the slave owners could not take away their rich tradition of storytelling or their imaginations. Slaves were forbidden to speak their native languages and to write, but they continued to tell stories. Some stories were based on memories, while others were based on new experiences and hopes.

Animals were often the heroes in African folktales. These heroes showed up again in this country in the stories told by slaves. The African jackal became the American fox, the African hare became the American rabbit, and the African tortoise became the American turtle. In some stories, animals and young children were made to be smart and strong because slave masters did not let the slaves show their intelligence. "Brer Rabbit" and "Wiley and the Hairy Man" are examples of this kind of cleverness.

Animals were also used to answer questions about nature. "How the Turtle Got Marks on Its Shell," "How the Sea Creatures Found Their Home," and "Why Spiders Have No Hair" are a few examples of this type of story.

Sometimes, stories told in slave cabins, around campfires, or in underground hideouts did more than entertain—they held hidden messages. "The People Could Fly" and "Follow the Drinking Gourd" had hidden messages telling slaves how to escape, how to hide, and who would help them. Some stories also taught valuable moral lessons. "The Talking Eggs" shows the importance of following directions and being respectful.

These stories were told from one generation to the next, and they passed along history, culture, hopes, and fears. The African American culture grew and expanded through these stories. The stories are so interesting that they can be enjoyed by both children and adults.

"Brer Rabbit Gets Brer Fox's Dinner"

One day Brer Rabbit was walking down the road by Brer Fox's house. Brer Fox was putting new shingles on his roof. In the yard was Brer Fox's dinner. Brer Rabbit knew that there was more food in the basket than in his own stomach. He also knew he couldn't beat Brer Fox in a fight, so he'd have to think of another way to get that dinner.

"Hey, Brer Fox," Brer Rabbit said, "what are you doing?"

"I'm putting new shingles on my roof," Brer Fox answered.

"Can I help?" Brer Rabbit asked.

"OK," Brer Fox said, "but I'm not sure you'll be much help."

Brer Rabbit started to hammer nails into the shingles. He was fast. In no time, the roof was finished. Brer Fox was very happy with his new worker. That is, until he realized that Brer Rabbit had nailed his tail to the roof.

"Rabbit," yelled Brer Fox, "unnail my tail!"

"Gee," said Rabbit, climbing down the ladder, "I've never nailed a tail before. I must be losing my aim. Maybe my eyesight is getting weak. How could I have nailed his tail? Making a mistake like that always makes me hungry."

So while Brer Fox continued to holler, a grinning Brer Rabbit enjoyed a fine dinner.

"Wiley and the Hairy Man"

One day a long time ago, a boy named Wiley was sent to gather sticks by the Tombigbee River in Alabama. "Take your hound dogs because the Hairy Man will get you if you don't," said Wiley's mom.

When he got to the Tombigbee River, Wiley's hound dogs ran off to chase a rabbit. A minute later, the Hairy Man came. Wiley climbed up a tree. The Hairy Man took an ax out of his bag and started chopping down the tree.

"Fly chips fly," yelled Wiley. "Fly back to your own places."

Sure enough, the wood chips flew back into place. The Hairy Man chopped faster, and Wiley yelled louder. But the Hairy Man was winning. Then Wiley heard his dogs barking. He called them, and they chased the Hairy Man back to the swamp.

When he got home, Wiley was still scared. His mom gave him some advice.

"Next time, tie up the dogs," said his mother. "Tell the Hairy Man that you know he is the best magician around."

So the next time Wiley went to the Tombigbee River, he tied up his dogs. Soon he saw the Hairy Man coming through the trees swinging a sack. The Hairy Man was smiling because he knew Wiley had lost his dogs. Wiley wanted to run, but he was scared stiff. "Hello,

Hairy Man," Wiley said. "I hear you're the best magician around here."

"I am," said the Hairy Man.

"I bet you can't turn yourself into a gorilla," said Wiley.

"Sure I can," said the Hairy Man. And he turned himself into a gorilla.

"I bet you can't turn into a lion," said Wiley.

"Oh yeah?" said the Hairy Man. And he turned himself into a lion.

"Anybody can make themselves big," said Wiley. "I bet you can't turn into a mouse!"

"Oh yeah?" said the Hairy Man. And he turned himself into a mouse.

Then Wiley picked him up, threw him in the bag, and tossed the bag into the river. Wiley felt happy, but he knew the Hairy Man would be back.

"We fooled the Hairy Man two times," said his mother. "If we fool him three times, he will never come back."

Wiley's mom made him bring her a young pig from the pen. She put the pig in Wiley's bed and had Wiley hide in the loft.

Wiley heard the Hairy Man climbing up onto the roof. He tried to go down the chimney, but he couldn't because it was too hot. Then the Hairy Man jumped down, knocked on the door, and asked for Wiley.

"You can't have him, Hairy Man," said Wiley's mom.

The Hairy Man thought of a couple more tricks to try to get Wiley, but every time his mother outsmarted him. Finally, Wiley's mom said, "If I do give you the young'un, will you go away?" The Hairy Man swore he would.

When the Hairy Man got to the bed and pulled back the covers, he found a young pig. "I never said which young'un I'd give you," said Wiley's mom.

Gritting his teeth, the Hairy Man huffed and puffed and cursed, as he went away with the young pig. Wiley and his mother had fooled the Hairy Man three times. Now he would never come back.

"How the Turtle Got Marks on Its Shell"

One day, a turtle was out with his wife. They were poor and hungry. "Today is the town's market day," said the husband turtle. "We shall go and buy some food."

The turtle's wife knew they had no money. She hoped that some day she and her husband could get food. She then noticed her husband admiring several eagles flying around.

"I wish that I could eat as often as those eagles," said the husband turtle.

The eagles overheard him. "We would be happy to carry you to our king up in the clouds," said the eagles. "He will feed you."

Filled with joy, the husband turtle accepted and was taken high in the air. But he forgot to invite his wife.

"Who is the food for?" asked the turtle.

"For everyone," one eagle replied.

"Let us all choose names for ourselves," said the turtle, who considered himself to be very wise.

The eagles chose human names, but the Turtle chose the name "Everyone."

When the eagles and the turtle were on the clouds, the king eagle came out with bowls of wonderful fruits and meats. Turtle also noticed all sorts of other foods.

"Who is the food for?" Turtle cried.

"For everyone," said the king.

So the turtle claimed all the food because his name was Everyone.

When the turtle was done eating, he said to the eagles, "Fly down to my wife and tell her to lay down some soft things for me to land on when I fall from here."

Because the turtle had been so greedy, the eagles did just the opposite. They told Turtle's wife to put down broken bottles, rocks, and all sorts of hard things.

When the turtle jumped down, he hit his shell on all the glass and rocks. That's how the turtle got marks on its

shell. Even today, turtles have marks on their shells as a reminder of the turtle's greediness.

"How the Sea Creatures Found Their New Home"

Many years ago in the forest, sea creatures wandered around on the land. There were fish, octopuses, sea horses, and eels, but they didn't have a home or a place to call their own. They went in search of a new home with their leader, the King Blue Whale.

The creatures packed their things and walked and walked and walked until they came to a beautiful yellow land. They wanted to stay there. "This land is beautiful!" said one Octopus.

"Is this our new home?" asked the Sea Horses.

They were resting in the new land when a mean lion came. He roared at them and told them to leave. "This land is mine," roared the lion. "I'm not going to share it with any sea creatures."

The King Blue Whale told them all to be patient. The animals walked and walked and walked until they found another beautiful place. "This land is be-yoooo-ti-ful!" said the King Blue Whale.

"Is this our new home?" asked the Sea Horses.

It was a pretty green land. The Whale looked around, but just as he was about to say "Yes," he heard a horrible, loud, awful screeching noise. A gray elephant lumbered up. "What are you creatures doing here?" he demanded.

"We are looking for a new land," answered the King Blue Whale.

"Well, you cannot stay here," said the elephant. "This is my home, the land of the Elephants. You must move on."

"Where are we going to live now?" asked the Fish.

The creatures packed up their things again, and they walked and walked and walked. "How much farther do we have to go?" asked the Eels.

By this time they were so tired, they were losing their legs. They looked around. This new land was beautiful. It was quiet. It was blue. There was no lion and no elephant. Now they were not walking *on* the land, they were floating through it. It was water.

"Is this our new home?" asked the Sea Horses.

The King Blue Whale looked around. He looked left. He looked right. He looked up. He looked down. Then he grinned a big whale grin. "Yes!" he said. "This is our land and will always be our land." And so the Sea Creatures had found their new home—the ocean.

"Why Spiders Have No Hair"

Anansi the spider lived in a village in Africa. He was a show-off. He liked people to think that he was the best. When his mother-in-law died, he wanted to act sadder than anyone else. He decided not to eat for eight days. Anansi knew he would get hungry, so before he went to the funeral, he stuffed his face. After the

funeral, his family had a feast, but he refused to eat anything. He announced to everyone, "I say what I mean, and I mean what I say. I will not eat until the eighth day."

On the third day, his family went out into the field to gather food. They left Anansi in charge of the large pot of baked beans. He was so hungry, he couldn't take it any more. He scooped up a big cupful of hot beans. Just when he was about to take a bite, he saw his family coming back. He had to hide the beans fast, so he dumped them into his hat and put it back on. The beans were hot on his head, so he started to shake his hat. When his family saw him, they asked what was wrong. He quickly thought of an excuse. "In my village, today is the hat-shaking festival," he said. "So I'm shaking my hat. I think I should go to the festival."

He started to leave, still dancing and shaking his hat, but his family followed him so that they could join in the

festival, too. When the hot beans on his head had burned off all his hair—and he didn't think he could take it any more—Anansi threw off his hat. His family picked it up and saw the hot beans. They started laughing.

Anansi jumped into the tall grass to hide himself. That's why spiders often hide in tall grass and don't have a single hair on their heads.

"The People Could Fly"

Once a woman called Sarah was beaten to the ground and couldn't get up again. Her baby cried, so it was whipped by the driver. If slaves didn't work hard and fast, they were beaten until they bled. A wise magic man named Toby said magic words to help the slaves fly to freedom. Only the strong could fly. Only those who had faith in their ability to escape could fly.

"Kum ya li kum buba tambe," Toby said. These words made them fly. The slaves forgot their native language because they weren't allowed to speak it,

but they still remembered enough to make them fly.

The owners tried to beat down the flying slaves, but it didn't work. Toby followed the flying slaves. He was magic, and he was God's helper. The slave driver wanted to kill Toby, but he couldn't. Toby laughed at him. "We are the ones who fly!" he said.

Not all of the slaves were able to fly, because they didn't have enough faith. The people who couldn't fly told their children about the people who could fly.

• • • • •

Flying in this story has two meanings. Strong faith (flying) helped the slaves be free in spirit even when they were working. It also took strong faith to "fly" or escape to freedom. This story offers hope that all people can be free and respected.

"Follow the Drinking Gourd"

During the time of slavery, stories had hidden messages to help slaves escape.

Peg Leg Joe and other legendary underground railroad conductors worked as handymen for different plantation owners. At night they would teach the slaves a story that gave directions for escaping. The slaves began singing this story, "Follow the Drinking Gourd." Here are some of the words to the song: "Follow the drinking gourd / The riverbank makes a very good road / The dead trees will show you the way / Left foot, peg foot, traveling on / The river ends between two hills / There's another river on the other side / When the great big river meets the little river, follow the drinking gourd / For the old man is a-waiting for to carry you to freedom if you follow the drinking gourd."

Many versions of this story have been written down. All of them agree that there is a code in the song. The drinking gourd was the Big Dipper, which pointed to the North Star and the way to freedom. Escaping slaves were warned to travel by river. They looked for a footprint and a peg print on dead trees that marked the path. The Tombigbee River, which starts in Alabama, was the "river that ends between two hills." Next they would come to "the river on the other side," or the Tennessee River.

As their journey continued, they would meet the old man waiting to carry them to freedom at the great big river. If they made it that far, Peg Leg Joe or another helper would escort them across the Ohio River into the free states and to an "underground railroad station." These stations were often houses or barns with secret rooms in which to hide the escaping slaves.

The slaves' journey was still dangerous and frightening until they were able to cross Lake Erie into Canada. Anywhere along the way, they could have been caught and returned to their owners. Once in Canada, they were really free.

"The Talking Eggs"

Way before you were born, there was a shabby house in the woods. An old woman lived there with her two daughters, Blanche and Rose. Blanche was as sweet as sugar, very generous, and always willing to help around the house. Rose was terribly spoiled, greedy, and stingy and thought only of herself. Their mother liked Rose best because she and Rose were so much alike. They were very mean to Blanche and made her do all the work around the house. Rose and her mother always dreamed of going to the city to be grand ladies.

On a hot day, the mother sent Blanche to the well to get water because

Rose was thirsty. After filling the bucket, Blanche saw an old woman in a dark black shawl. The woman asked kindly for a sip of water. Blanche, being very kind, said "Yes, ma'am." To repay Blanche's kindness, the old woman invited her to her shack to spend the night and have dinner. The old woman made Blanche promise not to laugh at anything she saw at her house.

The first thing Blanche saw was a two-headed cow with corkscrews for horns. She also saw chickens of all colors with different numbers of legs. These chickens whistled instead of clucking. Although these things were strange, Blanche kept her promise and didn't laugh at any of it.

While they were inside, the old woman asked Blanche to light a fire and start supper. All there was to put in the pot of water was an old beef bone, which magically turned into stew. The old woman also gave Blanche one grain of rice, which turned into many grains of rice as soon as it was ground. Just when Blanche thought nothing could be stranger, the old woman took off her head and started braiding her hair. When she finished, she put her head back on.

The next morning Blanche went to milk the two-headed cow, which gave her the sweetest-tasting milk she had ever had. Next, she collected the eggs. The old woman had told her to collect only those eggs that said "take me" and to leave the ones that said "don't take me." As it turned out, the ones that said "don't take me" were jeweled and colorful. The ones that said "take me" were just plain white eggs. Blanche was tempted to take the pretty ones, but she obeyed the old woman.

As she was leaving, the old woman promised Blanche that things would get better for her and her family. She told her to throw the eggs over her left shoulder, one at a time, as she walked home. When she did this, the eggs became beautiful dresses, shoes, diamonds, rubies, and even a horse and carriage.

When Blanche got home with all her newfound riches, her mother and sister were very jealous—so jealous, in fact, that after questioning Blanche, her mother sent Rose off to find the old woman and get more.

Rose found the old woman, but things did not turn out the same way. Rose laughed at the strange animals, refused to cook, received sour milk from the cow, and took the eggs that said "don't take me."

On her way home, each time she threw an egg over her right shoulder, something terrible came out. She tried running home, but the snakes, lizards, and wolves followed her. Her mom heard her yelling and tried to save her, but the animals chased them both into the woods.

When they finally made it back home, Blanche had left for the city to become a grand lady. She remained as kind and loving as always.

The moral of this story is: It pays to respect people's differences and not make fun of them.

LANGUAGE

Language is a very powerful tool. Slave owners hoped to keep slaves powerless by outlawing their African languages. White owners believed that if the slaves only spoke English, they could not use their naive language to make secret plans. At the same time, slaves were severely punished for speaking "formal" English. They were accused of learning to read or being "uppity."

To avoid appearing "uppity," the slaves developed their own language system and sentence structure. This new language became known as Black English. Black English grew out of the need to communicate without the white community being able to understand. Blacks combined both African and American words to form codes and passwords that only other slaves could understand. When slaves spoke to each other, the white master heard one thing, but the slaves often meant something else.

Black English is still spoken today, but many African Americans think it is important to be bilingual. Black English is often used around peers, family members, and others within the black community. Formal English is used in school and work settings.

Many expressions and sayings have been passed from one generation to the next. Certain expressions, originally considered black slang, are now common in mainstream America. How often do you use the word "OK"? Some people say it originated from the African words *Yaw Kay*.

LITERATURE

While much African American history is still passed down orally, it is also being written down. Slaves sometimes risked their lives to learn to write. It was the narratives of escaped slaves that helped others work to stop slavery. Many black authors are being published in the twentieth century. Their work records all aspects of African American life. These are just a few of the outstanding books for children by African American authors who have earned awards for literary achievement. Look for these and other books at your local bookstore or public library.

Roll of Thunder, Hear my Cry by Mildred D. Taylor (New York: Dial Books, 1976). This story shares the struggles of a young African American girl as she grows up.

Fallen Angels by Walter Dean Myers (New York: Scholastic Inc., 1988). Mr. Myers wrote this book in memory of his brother who died in Vietnam.

Mufaro's Beautiful Daughters by John Steptoe, illustrated by John Steptoe (New York: Lothrop, Lee & Shepard Books, 1987). This is a story of two beautiful daughters competing to be queen.

Nathaniel Talking by Eloise Greenfield, illustrated by Jan Spivey Gilchrist (New York: Black Butterfly Children's Books, 1988). This book is about a kid named Nathaniel and his rap poems. He is able to speak through his rapping.

Aunt Flossie's Hats by Elizabeth Fitzgerald Howard, paintings by James Ransome (New York: Clarion Books, 1991). A grandmother tells her grandchildren a story from her childhood.

REAL PEOPLE

Ministers, artists, and lots of others,
Children, fathers, sisters, and brothers.
The more they say, the more you learn.
It takes all people to make the world turn.

We are very proud of this section. We feel it has some of the most important information in the entire book. It's important because it comes from real people—people just like you and me. They come from neighborhoods, schools, homes, places, and experiences that are the same as yours and mine. They have been generous enough to answer a list of our questions, plus they told us even more than we could have hoped. They shared their life stories with us as well as their values and goals, providing information that you can't generally find in books. This information comes from the heart and soul.

The real people that you will read about have two main things in common: One, they are African American. Two, they never gave up. When they ran into a problem, they persisted until they overcame it.

Although these people are of different backgrounds, have different occupations, and are from different parts of the country, you will find a common thread running through their lives. Their families stressed education and a belief in God as keys to success. In their lives, we think you'll be able to find valuable lessons, as well as some interesting stories.

We hope you'll learn a lot and enjoy them as much as we have.

DARYL PRICE

Daryl Price is 6 feet 5 inches tall and weighs 254 pounds. He plays outside linebacker. Because he was quite talented when he played football for a high school in Beaumont, Texas, he earned a scholarship to play football for the University of Colorado Buffaloes. Even though Mr. Price has a chance to make a career in football, he feels his education is more important to him than his athletic career. If he were to get hurt, his football career could be over. His main goal is to receive degrees in molecular biology and religious studies.

Daryl was born on October 23, 1972, in Galveston, Texas. He has two younger brothers, ages 11 and 13, and an older sister who is 21. He recalls having to deal with a full house all the time because his cousins often came to stay with them.

Daryl feels that education is the key to fighting racial discrimination. "I get mad at the thing, not at the person," Daryl said, when asked about prejudice. "I try to learn more because I don't want people to have the idea that African Americans can't learn or aren't intelligent. The media contributes to putting people in these categories."

Daryl looks up to Martin Luther King Jr. because Dr. King believed in something and stuck with it right to his death. Daryl tries to apply this to himself. At one point, he went through some tough times in his life. He began to wonder why he didn't feel smart. Then he

Daryl Price

met an intelligent African American girl ranked second in their class. From that point on, Daryl Price decided you can't use being black as an excuse. You have to decide what you're going to do and do it.

When Daryl was growing up, his parents weren't always able to visit school, or go to awards nights, or see his football games. It's not that they didn't care, they just didn't have the time. They worked all day and night to pay the bills and to clothe and feed their children. His family taught him that there is always a right way and a wrong way. Even if it might take longer to do something the right way, it's better than doing something the wrong way. The family always spent Sundays together and attended church.

Daryl's best advice for kids is, first, trust in God. Second, get an education and don't let people tell you what you can or can't accomplish. Daryl Price is an African American who is willing to do what it takes to get where he wants and needs to be.

DOROTHY JENKINS FIELDS

"It is important for African American youth to study and explore the history of their heritage," says Dorothy Jenkins Fields. "With this knowledge, they can work on the problems of today to make a better world."

On New Year's Eve, 1942, Dorothy Jenkins Fields was born in Miami, Florida. Her grandparents had moved to Miami from the Bahamas in 1903. She was an only child with lots of cousins. As a little girl, she loved to listen to her two aunts and four uncles while they entertained her grandmother with jokes and family stories. Mrs. Fields' mother inspired her to strive to do the best she could. "My mother is the wind beneath my wings," she said.

During the 1940s, African Americans were called "colored" people. As Mrs. Fields grew up, they became known as "Negroes." In the late 1960s, some people began calling themselves "black." Still later, blacks started to choose what they wanted to be called. In the 1970s, the name changed to "Afro-American," but today most people use the title "African American." Dorothy Jenkins Fields believes it is important to be able to choose a name for yourself and not have others tell you who you are. She still calls herself an Afro American.

Mrs. Fields is married and has two daughters, Katherine and Edda. Katherine is a graduate of Spelman College and is studying for her master's degree in business administration. Edda is a senior at Emory University, studying in Sierra Leone, West Africa.

One day, Mrs. Fields went to the library to read about local African Americans. The clerk told her they only had a folder with obituaries, which are notices of people who have died. When Mrs. Fields asked why, the clerk said, "I guess those people have not thought enough of themselves to write their own history." Mrs. Fields disagreed and realized the need to collect and organize information so that books could be written about African Americans in Miami. She hopes to develop a program in which African American youths become actively involved in recording their own ethnic heritage and sharing it with others.

Mrs. Fields started the black archives in Miami. An archive is a place to keep important papers. Because Mrs. Fields runs the archives, she is called an archivist. The black archives contain the

Dorothy Jenkins Fields

histories and important papers of people in Miami's black community. They also have reference books, architectural drawings, oral history tapes, sound recordings, exhibits, slides, videotapes, and newspapers.

Miami is very fortunate to have the talented Dorothy Jenkins Fields, a social studies specialist and archivist in the Dade County Public Schools, helping African American people understand their heritage and live better lives.

Leon Smith

LEON SMITH

Leon Smith is an African American who has dedicated 26 years of his life to the military. Mr. Smith represents a large number of African Americans who have served our country in war and peace. He believes the most important things in his life are bonding with his family and getting a good education. Mr. Smith's family, like many others, contains mixed heritages. One of his grandfathers was part Irish, and another was a Cherokee who grew up on an Indian reservation in Oklahoma.

As a child, Mr. Smith's favorite role model was Nat King Cole, because he wanted to be a singer. He has two younger brothers and one older sister, and he loves his family very much. Mr. Smith was born on January 30, 1928, in Maple Hill, Kansas. The town only had 208 people in it. Church played a very big role in his family life, and they had to walk four miles every Sunday to attend.

At school, he got good grades, but he was often teased because he was one of the only African American kids there.

Mr. Smith has done many things in his life. He has been in the army for three wars and has worked as a hotel cook and a singer. His truck battalion was the first to enter Berlin in the Second World War. They went through "the Berlin Corridor," which, he said, was very scary. He was very troubled by the way African Americans were treated in the service. They fought and died beside the white soldiers every day, but they were separated in their living quarters until a 1949 law forced the military to integrate. He fought in an artillery unit in the Korean War. He also fought in the Vietnam War.

Mr. Smith has always been very active in the Baptist church, even when he lived in different countries around the world. When he was a soldier in Korea, he helped a missionary. They worked in a leper colony. Normally, no one was allowed to visit leper colonies, but Mr. Smith did.

A person who stands out in Mr. Smith's mind as being very special was Mr. Krammer, a white man. Mr. Krammer gave him his first job as a fry cook and always treated him fairly. Mr. Krammer was like a father to him.

Mr. Smith says that school helped him achieve success. Education was important to him. His wife was also very important in his life. When she died at the age of 45, he raised his three girls and two boys by himself. Mr. Smith feels that parents are models for children, and he has tried to teach his children the value of religion, responsibility, and education. "Families stay together and work together," he said. He feels blessed that he has eight grandchildren. Family celebrations are his favorite memories, especially Christmas, Thanksgiving, New Year's, and the Fourth of July (his sister's birthday).

Being an African American growing up in small towns in Kansas, Mr. Smith remembers being called "Jim Crow." Whenever he was teased, he walked away and ignored his teaser rather than fight. As a child, his brothers and sister helped him solve problems in other ways than by fighting. When they were young, they liked to dance. They danced on a small platform outside the dance hall, but it was forbidden to dance with white people. Prejudice was strong while Mr. Smith was growing up.

Mr. Smith's feelings about equality are very strong. He feels that many jobs are not given to blacks, even when they are very qualified. Today, he is retired from the army. He keeps active by taking care of his grandchildren. Mr. Smith said if he could change one thing in the world, there would be more education about different cultures in the school. This way, people could see that everyone is equal.

GEORGETTE AJULUFOH

Georgette Ajulufoh is an African American who sees her people as smart and strong. As a bright young woman engineer, she thinks African Americans must educate themselves if they want to do well in life. She would also like to help educate other African Americans and start her own company someday.

Mrs. Ajulufoh is an example of what a good family can provide. She was born in Jackson, Mississippi, on July 29, 1963, surrounded by good education and excellent role models. Georgette's parents were strict but loving and were strong influences in her life. They taught her to live by the Bible, to treat people equally, to get a good education, and to have high moral standards. They also taught her how to behave, because they knew their daughter's behavior would represent them.

As an independent-minded woman, Georgette made two major decisions in her young life. One was to leave home after graduating from college, and the other was to get married. She decided to leave Mississippi so she could be on her own. Her husband is from the African

Georgette Ajulufoh

country of Nigeria. Before she met him, she thought Africa was like she had seen in the movies. After meeting and getting to know her husband and learning about his country and culture, she now realizes that there are many similarities between his African homeland and her southern roots in the United States.

While Georgette lived on the farmlands of Mississippi, she learned that family ties are more important than anything else. She has a deep appreciation for close relationships and family values. Her father was her first hero. He was a big and strong man. He protected his family and always showed his two daughters that life held lots of challenges. He died when Georgette was ten years old. Her mother then became the family's strength, working two jobs to support the family. Mrs. McKenzie, Georgette's mother, gave her two daughters the help and encouragement they needed to be successful. Georgette became strong and independent. You can see why her parents are her role models.

As a child, Georgette and her younger sister, Phyllis, were encouraged to stay in school and to get a good education. Georgette went to Jackson State University in Mississippi, earning a bachelor's degree in computer science. She now has a job as a systems engineer in Troy, Michigan, where she designs and writes computer programs for EDS, a branch of General Motors Corporation.

Mrs. Ajulufoh remembers that in seventh grade, two boys picked on her because of her color. It was a hard time for her. She didn't want to go to school, and she couldn't stop the teasing. She felt bad inside and lost much of her self-esteem. Mrs. Ajulufoh worked extra hard to prove that she was better than the people who picked on her. She thinks that people should be judged by their character or personality, not their race.

As an African American woman, Mrs. Ajulufoh thinks she has always worked harder to prove that she is as good as the next person. If she had the chance to make a positive change for our society, she would wish for people to be color-blind. She would also like all young African Americans to "educate themselves." Kids should "stay in school, learn as much as they can, and be the best they can possibly be."

FRANK HUGHES

Hundreds of people flooded into the little Catholic church in New Jersey to pay their last respects to Frank Hughes. Even

Elaine Hughes, Mr. Hughes' wife of 45 years, was surprised that so many people attended the funeral. "I didn't know my husband knew so many people," she said.

Until his death in 1994, Frank Hughes had dedicated most of his life to helping others. He did this in spite of losing both of his legs in 1963 while helping his friend avoid an oncoming car. Even though he was a paraplegic for more than 30 years, Mr. Hughes never stopped reaching out to others.

After the funeral, Mrs. Hughes told us a little bit about her husband. Frank Hughes was born into a large family on January 21, 1919, in Augusta, Georgia. He barely knew his mother because she died when he was young. He went to New York to live with his Uncle Frank in the Bronx. When Mr. Hughes was older, he was drafted into the air force. Before he went off to fight in World War II, he met his wife at a friend's wedding and they married soon after.

In the air force, Mr. Hughes worked hard and became an officer. The air force provided an opportunity for both him and his wife to travel many places. His last assignment was as a Senior Master Sergeant at McGuire Air Force Base in New Jersey. After more than 20 years in the Air Force, Mr. Hughes' career ended when he had the terrible accident in which he lost both his legs.

During the two years Mr. Hughes was in the hospital, his faith helped him take a closer look at his life. As soon as he was able to handle the changes in his own life, he tried to help others in the hospital. He talked to the young service-men who were hospitalized because of the Vietnam War. Many of these men had injuries that were even worse than his. He would tell the young people in the hospital to trust in God, get an educa-tion, and be responsible for their behav-ior. Even while he was in pain, Mr. Hughes was always kind to other people.

When Mr. Hughes first came home from the hospital, he became very depressed because he had so much time and nothing to do. This made Mrs. Hughes sad, too. She told her boss about her husband's situation, and he offered Mr. Hughes a job. While doing this job, Mr. Hughes passed the Civil Service Test, which helped him get a job working for the U.S. government. Soon he was hired for a civil service position during a time when it was difficult for disabled people to find jobs.

Most of us take for granted things like having a job or being able to walk around whenever we want. For Mr. Hughes, these things presented many

Frank and Elaine Hughes

challenges. He helped his community recognize the need for designated parking areas for the handicapped and easier ways for people in wheelchairs to get into buildings. Mr. and Mrs. Hughes worked hard during their many years of volunteer service. They visited hospitals and collected food and money for the needy, especially at Thanksgiving. He loved to help the less fortunate in his community. Even though Frank Hughes was disabled, he cared for others, and took time to thank God every day. In 1971, he received the "Handicapped Person of the Year Award" for his commitment to improving the lives of handicapped people everywhere.

SYLVIA KIRK

Sylvia Kirk wants to be accepted for who she is—"a black African American woman." Mrs. Kirk throws textbooks out the window so that kids can actually live history. She is an intelligent and creative teacher who works in Midwest City, Oklahoma. After talking with her, we would love to have her for our teacher.

Mrs. Kirk's mother was a high-school graduate. She went on to college, but left to get married. Her father was a construction worker. After her parents divorced, Sylvia grew up in an extended family with her grandparents, mother, and cousins. The divorce affected Sylvia later on in her teens. Even though her mother remarried, she still was hurt that she did not have her real father around

Sylvia Kirk

like other kids did. She cared deeply for her stepfather, but he still wasn't her real father. She grew up in New York and the Catskill Mountains. She lived in mixed neighborhoods with Jewish, white, and black people. She liked to go outside and jump rope, which was popular at that time.

Sometimes at night her grandmother would go out on the porch and tell her stories about the past. Some of the stories were about her grandfather and his experiences as a sharecropper. He leased or rented land from another person, and at the end of the year, he and his partner would split the profits of the harvested crop. Mrs. Kirk's grandmother sang old spirituals and spoke of hardships she had lived through. These hardships didn't bother her because she believed all people have to deal with hardships in their lives. Mrs. Kirk thought so much about this that later, when she became a teacher, she wrote a play about her grandparents' life, which her students performed.

Her mother and grandmother worked very hard to teach Sylvia to be proud of her heritage and who she is. It wasn't until she went to school that she discovered prejudice. She remembered that her teachers sometimes placed students in a group because of their skin color. These students didn't have a chance to study the way they wanted. Sylvia's mom was different, and she made sure that the teachers challenged her daughter.

Mrs. Kirk thinks that God and her family are the most important things in her life. At Thanksgiving, they thank God for the blessings He has given their family. These values came from her mother and grandmother, who are her heroines.

Mrs. Kirk has been married more than 20 years. Her husband was a major in the air force. He was a mission crew commander and worked with reconnaissance planes, which are planes that take secret pictures. They have three children. Dana is 9, Shoan is 12, and Rhyan is 14.

Mrs. Kirk believes that people should be called what they want to be called. She wants to be thought of as an African American. She also believes that no one should think that other people are bad because their skin is a different color. Being African American is wonderful, even though there are many difficulties because of color. People tend to lump African Americans together, which is not fair to them. African Americans are a people with a rich heritage. Mrs. Kirk wishes that we had a color-blind society in which all people would be treated equally.

Mrs. Kirk told us that we should try to get an education and to strive for excellence. Kids should make goals so that they know where they are going, and work hard to get there. She believes it's hard for people to ignore you or treat you unfairly when you are the best!

RODNEY JONES

"The soul inside of me has no color," says Rodney Jones. "Everybody's soul has the same color."

Rodney Jones was born on August 30, 1956, in New Haven, Connecticut. As a nine-year-old, he enjoyed going to Palisades Amusement Park with his father and friends. He loved the cotton candy and hot dogs. When he wasn't at the amusement park, he and his friends played hide-and-seek around the seminary where his father was the dean.

At a young age, Rodney played in a band with his good friend Jackie Byard. Once, Rodney wrote a song called "Gaze." Like other songwriters, he sat by the radio hoping his song would be played. After four months, he finally heard his song. He loves his guitar, but sometimes he plays the electric bass, too. Bruce Johnson, a jazz guitarist, is also a good friend and a wonderful role model who taught Randy to find the creative spark within himself. Mr. Jones now

Rodney Jones

works as a music teacher at the Manhattan School of Music. He teaches music composition and gives guitar lessons.

Mr. Jones loves his family very much. His parents taught him to have a strong sense of what is right and wrong and to believe that all people are a gift from God. His father told him that words and actions should be the same, but actions should come before words. Mr. Jones wants to inherit his father's honesty, self-discipline, and self-control, and he also wants to be appreciated by people around him.

Mr. Jones loves to eat. Some of his favorite foods are sushi (raw fish), chicken, barbecue, ribs, frozen fruit juices, and popsicles. He thinks his mom is the best cook in the world. "But, of course," he says, "everyone thinks that."

Leana Mitchell, Serena Lynn, and Laura Alia are Mr. Jones's three loving daughters and his pride and joy. Leana wants to be a writer and teacher, and Serena and Laura want to be veterinarians when they grow up.

Mr. Jones has lived his whole life trying to accept and learn new things every day. He takes it slow but learns quickly. His belief in God is strong, and he prays every day. He is kind and warmhearted, helping many African Americans learn about their culture. He wants to share his music with everyone.

BILL POTTS

Bill Potts believes people are both different and alike in many ways. He thinks people should be treated equally and fairly. From a very young age, Bill Potts was very artistic. As a child, he would build things out of cardboard, wood, and other scraps that he found. Today he is a folk artist who sells his carvings across the country.

Mr. Potts has been married for 32 years and lives and works in the Denver area. He was born March 22, 1936, in Des Moines, Iowa. Like many African Americans, Mr. Potts has different heritages. His father was three-fourths Native American, and his mother was an African American. Mr. Potts can trace his family tree back to the time of slavery. His grandmother was a slave.

After earning a scholarship to Drake University, Mr. Potts dropped out during his junior year to join the army. He stayed in the army for 20 years. Mr. Potts was the only African American in his platoon when he served in Vietnam. When confronted by racial discrimination, he didn't let it get to him. Once when he was in the service, he had to sit in the back of the bus because he was African American. He couldn't figure out why he had to do this. After all, he had paid the same amount of money as all of the other guys had.

Mr. Potts is a folk artist. When he travels in his car, he stops and picks up wood from the side of the road. He never lets a piece of wood go to waste. He also recycles, turning hunks of junk into works of art. He carves many things, like animals, rocket ships, walking sticks, and people. He also enjoys going to the movies and flying his cardboard airplanes in his spare time.

A man with a strong belief in God, Mr. Potts is making sacrifices to follow his dream. He goes without a lot of extras like fancy clothes and cars because he doesn't always have the money to buy them. He donates his time and artwork to many worthy causes. Mr. Potts spent the entire day with us at our workshop. He gave us a wooden fish that he made right in front of our eyes. He started with four old two-by-fours that had been glued together. He used a saw to start carving the wood. We began to see the shape develop. Some of the tools he used were a rasp, which is like a large file, a saw, and other power tools. After we saw the shape of the fish, he painted the fish using bright red, blue, and white colors. These colors are used by many folk artists. He left this beautiful fish for us to enjoy. Each time we see it, we'll remember a man who is artistic and sincere about his work. Mr. Potts taught us never to give up on our dreams, and to dedicate our time and effort to our dreams and goals. He is a kind, caring, funny, and hardworking man.

CARNEICE BROWN WHITE

Carneice Brown White was born in Memphis, Tennessee, on June 22, 1929. Her father was a Pullman porter for the railroad, and her mother was a caterer and homemaker. She has one older sister. Carneice's family lived in Memphis until she was nine years old. Then they moved to Denver.

Mrs. White is married to Matthew Lee White, a realtor and employee of the Denver Bulk Mail Center. She has two children who are now adults. Her son, Drusel, is a musical arranger and keyboard player. Cecilia Kay, her daughter,

Bill Potts

Carneice Brown White

was named the first African American "All-American Girl" in a contest. She also has a younger son named Omar, and she likes to play the harp.

Mrs. White retired after being a teacher for 40 years. In all those years of teaching, she has had a chance to see positive changes for African American children. But Mrs. White has not only seen change—she is usually the one who makes it happen.

After working with students for so many years, she saw that many of her inner-city students needed to have a place where learning could be fun. She wanted to teach her students how to eat in a fancy restaurant. She called the restaurant and told them what she needed. The manager of the restaurant let the kids eat for free! Since the restaurant was more than 100 miles away, Mrs. White got an airline to provide a plane for the kids to use! This was exciting for them because lots of the kids had never been in an airplane before. Mrs. White says that if you want the world to be a better place, every person has to do something. She says that if you're willing to ask, you'll find people who are willing to help you make a change. Because of her great teaching, Mrs. White was recognized as one of seven Outstanding Black Educators in America by the National Council for Negro Women.

Mrs. White helped continue a great tradition for the fifth graders at her school. Since the fifth-grade students would be leaving the elementary school to go to a junior high school the next year, she thought it was important for them to have a "continuation ceremony," which is like a graduation. The reason it's called a continuation ceremony is to remind the kids to continue in school, to graduate from high school, and maybe even college. Students dress up in their best clothes and march into the auditorium. While they are there, they listen to speakers, like Denver Mayor Wellington Webb, who tell the kids to keep learning and to finish school.

Mrs. White has retired, but she's not going to sit at home. She has already made plans to start an African American children's museum. She wants to teach all children about African American history. She wants the children to learn about black culture in a fun way and with understanding and friendship. One of the programs Mrs. White will have at the museum will be "The Magic of Goobers." This is a program in which

Mrs. White dresses up as Mrs. Goober and tells children about the contributions that African Americans have made to the United States. She is Mrs. Goober because "goober" is another name for the peanut, which came from Africa to the United States. The program is meant to build self-esteem and pride in young African Americans. Mrs. White was awarded a grant from the Public Service Company of Colorado to promote "The Magic of Goobers" across the country. This grant should help her reach her dream of opening the African American children's museum.

Because Mrs. White makes time to think of ideas for change, and since she has the strength to put them into action, her example has caused other people to take action. What can you do to make the world a better place? Don't forget what Mrs. White says—"If you are willing to ask, there are people willing to help."

PAUL STEWART

"You can't be a cowboy 'cause cowboys aren't black." This is what Paul Stewart heard every time he and his friends played cowboys and Indians.

Mr. Stewart is an African American cowboy. He was born on December 18, 1925, in Clinton, Iowa. His mother was three-fourths Native American. His father was African American. His father owned a trucking company and wanted his son to be a truck driver, too. "A winner never quits, and a quitter never wins," was something that Mr. Stewart's father said a lot. These are words that Mr. Stewart himself lives by today.

Through the years, Mr. Stewart was the only African American child in his school. Growing up in the North, he never knew the prejudice that African Americans in the South did. He remembers that once his father got stopped in Little Rock, Arkansas, while driving his truck down South. The police took his dad to the station and accused him of stealing the truck. "You can't own a truck," they told him. "You are not allowed to have property." His father

Paul Stewart

made many phone calls, and he finally proved the truck was his. This stuck in Mr. Stewart's mind, and his father became an excellent role model for him. He saw in his dad a person who didn't let others beat him down—he never quit.

Church also has played an important role in Mr. Stewart's life. He spent a lot of time praying during his youth. He would often ask his minister to pray for him and give him strength. After church, his family would often go on church outings. Mr. Stewart felt that these outings were important as well as fun. It is no surprise that his minister was also a role model for him. Mr. Stewart's family is very important to him. He has one sister and two brothers. He can trace his roots to author Alex Haley and famous athlete Jesse Owens. These people show that "a winner never quits, and a quitter never wins."

Mr. Stewart saw his first black cowboy when he moved to Denver. He was shocked because he never knew there

was such a thing. He read all he could about them and collected everything he could about the West, including boots, guns, spurs, and ropes. Whenever he met an African American cowboy, he would ask him questions, including if he would like to donate items to his cowboy collection. During his research, Mr. Stewart came up with another role model. He found a cowboy, Jesse Stahl, who represented not only strength but also creativity. Mr. Stahl would bring the rodeo crowd to its feet by riding his horse into the ring and having it fall on him. Usually the crowd thought Mr. Stahl was dead. After five minutes, he would slide out from under the horse, get up on the horse's back, and wave to the applauding crowd. In 1971, Mr. Stewart started the Black American West Museum and Heritage Center in Denver, Colorado.

Today, along with operating his museum, Mr. Stewart teaches African American history to students everywhere. He has written two books, *Westward Soul* and *Black Cowboys*. He plans to write three more books: *Black Music, Black Mining,* and *Black Women.* Many magazines and newspapers have written about Mr. Stewart and his achievements.

During his lifetime, Mr. Stewart has faced much racism. While in the service, he and a friend once went into a southern town and boarded a bus. He paid his fare. His friends went directly to the back of the bus, but he stood in the front. The bus driver had to ask him to move to the back. He didn't understand because he had paid the same fare as the other passengers. Another time, he went to get his shoes shined and sat down. All of the men doing the shining were white. Not one of them would come and help him. Another time, he went into a soda shop for a drink. The white owner told the African American man who was sweeping the floor to serve Mr. Stewart. Mr. Stewart turned to the white man and politely said, "No, thank you," and walked out.

Mr. Stewart believes fear is a big part of prejudice. He thinks prejudiced people don't feel good about themselves and pick on others to cover up their own bad feelings.

Mr. Stewart leaves us with this idea: Remember, to get something out of what you do, you must put yourself into it.

FATIMAH LINDA COLLIER JACKSON

Fatimah Jackson believes that challenges help people become stronger. This positive attitude has made her a happy and successful person. She is what her role models—her grandmother and her mother—would have called a "balanced" person. Her mother and grandmother taught her to be honest and creative and never to lose sight of her goals. Mrs. Jackson remembers that her grandmother always used leftovers to make another meal, never throwing out something useful. Later, Mrs. Jackson found this lesson in her Muslim belief that when there is

enough food for one, there is enough for two. This idea of sharing and sacrificing is important to Mrs. Jackson's life.

Fatimah Jackson was born on September 6, 1950, in Denver, Colorado. She grew up with her grandparents and other relatives in a large family. Her neighborhood included many different heritages: African American, Hispanic, and Japanese American. She remembers a happy childhood, but knows that segregation existed. People were allowed to live, eat, and work only in certain places.

Since her father died when she was six, her mother and grandmother took care of the family. Her favorite family times were vacations in the mountains. She loved playing with her cousins and remembers running up and down hills, drinking fresh spring water, riding in the back of a truck, visiting a dairy, and tasting ice-cold milk.

Mrs. Jackson's present home is Adelphi, Maryland, where she lives with her husband and six children. Family holidays revolve around the Muslim religion and African American celebrations such as Kwanzaa. Her name, Fatimah, was added when she became Muslim. Becoming a Muslim has helped her be a better person.

Mrs. Jackson finished her undergraduate education at Cornell University in Ithaca, New York, and was given an award for excellent achievement. She majored in science, later receiving her master's degree and her doctorate. While writing a long paper she had to write to receive her degree, she traveled to Africa to gather research. Now she is a professor of biological anthropology at the University of Maryland. Her husband is also a scientist.

Mrs. Jackson thinks her marriage has been one of the most important decisions she has made, since she has been married for more than 20 years. Two of her six children are in college, and the youngest is just three. Her family is close, and they depend on one another.

The first encounter with prejudice that she remembers came in a college classroom. Mrs. Jackson remembers that she felt the professor judged her by her color, not her ability. She had always been a good student, so she was surprised at first. Then she became angry. She made a point of telling her instructor early in a new semester that he would be receiving "A" work from her. She thinks that by turning the situation around, she gained her professor's respect and challenged herself to do her very best.

Mrs. Jackson bases her daily life on her religion. She wants the African American youth of today to follow the teachings of her elders: believe in yourself, do the best you can, and do everything you can to reach your goals.

The continent and people of Africa are very important to Mrs. Jackson. Africa is the homeland of humankind and the cradle of civilization. All people can learn from the rich history of Africa and Africans. The Qur'an (Koran)—the Muslim holy book—states that humans were created by God as different nations and tribes so that we would get to know each other, not so that we would dislike each other. This is one of the thoughts that guides her life.

STEVE FLOYD

Imagine a world in which we meet someone we know, and we become a part of each other's lives. The color of our skin doesn't make us good, but what counts is how we treat others. This is how Steve Floyd, a former gang member, wants the world to be.

Steve Floyd was born on Easter Sunday, March 29, 1959, in Chicago, Illinois. He feels that being born on Easter was special, because Easter is a day of sharing and accepting everyone no matter what color they are.

Mr. Floyd grew up in a one-parent family on the south side of Chicago. He was raised in the Robert Taylor Home projects, which was one of the poorest housing projects in the nation. He went through many hardships while he was growing up. His father had to leave his family to serve in the Vietnam War. When his father returned from Vietnam, his parents divorced. Later, his father was found dead in the street. His mother had to struggle to support Steve, his four brothers, and one sister. She was unable to spend much time with her children. Growing up without a father, Mr. Floyd turned to gangs for male acceptance and friendship. At age 17, he was shot by a rival gang member. He decided he had had enough of gang violence.

Steve Floyd

After Mr. Floyd gave up a career as a gang member, he moved on to bigger and better things. He went to college and earned a degree in theology and Biblical studies. He is now the Director of Outreach and Management with At High Risk Youth Services in Minneapolis, Minnesota. This program deals with inner-city street gangs. Mr. Floyd knows there are better things to get involved with than gang violence, because violence destroys people. He tries to motivate young people to live better lives.

Mr. Floyd thinks it's important to have friends. He knows from personal experience how strong the need to belong to something can be, but he warns kids that belonging to a violent gang can be deadly. He tells kids to remember that they always have choices in life. Kids need to make good choices, not bad ones. When your friends want you to do bad things, you shouldn't be afraid to be your own person and do your own thing.

When asked about racial discrimination, Mr. Floyd said it was a shock to him. When he was young, he lived in an all-black neighborhood and had hardly seen white people at all, except on television. The first time he realized that people judged others by the color of their skin was when he rode his bike into a white neighborhood. His bike broke, and he had to carry it out. While he was struggling to get the bike home, a white man accused him of stealing the bike and slapped him in the face.

This is a valuable lesson for all of us. Just because people look different, it doesn't mean they are doing bad things. Mr. Floyd thinks that African American people are special and that God is looking out for them. He says that African Americans need to understand their heritage and take pride in themselves. They also need to learn to love and accept one another.

Steve Floyd has three children named Steven, Chloe, and Josef. He told us that he is living for his kids first and other kids second. He believes that people need to provide activities for youth today, so they don't get involved in violent gangs. Our whole country needs to help solve the gang problem so that our streets and neighborhoods will be safe places to live.

KIDS WHO MAKE A DIFFERENCE

Being active, helping others—
That's a real hero.
Reaching for goals and never quitting—
That's a real hero.
Standing up for what is right—
That's a real hero.
Thinking of others and not just yourself—
That's a real hero.
Showing your best in all you do—
That's a real hero.

Heroes are everywhere—just look around you. Every day we live, play, and work with many unrecognized heroes. Real heroes don't need to have great looks, X-ray eyes, or super strength. They don't need to be rich or famous. You won't find them in comic books or in the movies either. A true hero is a real human being who is trying to make a difference.

Heroes speak every language, come in every color, and live in every country in the world. In this section, we want to introduce you to young African American heroes. These active young people volunteer to help in their com-munities and churches. They stand up for what is right, encouraging others to make wise decisions. When they help you, they make you feel good about yourself. We hope these stories help you recognize the heroes who live around you. If you decide to make a difference in your community, you'll be a hero, too.

TWYLA RIVERS

Everyone in the math class at Columbine Elementary was watching the clock. Something special was about to happen, and they could hardly wait. Finally, the teacher dismissed them, and the stu-

Twyla Rivers

dents ran to their homeroom. A news camera team was already there. This was exciting! A classmate, Twyla Rivers, was receiving the Channel 9 Kids Who Care Award. Often described as a "sparkling star," Twyla won the award because she uses her leadership skills to help others.

Twyla and her brother Greg live with their great-grandparents on the east side of Denver. The family lives in a large old house with a red roof and a big backyard. The great-grandparents have raised three generations of children in this house. Twyla's friends love to come visit. They play games and listen to rap music. Even if she isn't there, her friends feel free to stop in for a chat.

Twyla helps many people, and her great-grandpa is one of them. Twyla and her great-grandpa have lots in common because they both have a sense of humor. They also worry about things. Her great-grandpa has Parkinson's disease, which is an illness that affects the

nervous system. People with this problem often shake or move slowly. Twyla's great-grandpa has to take special medicine to control the disease. Sometimes the medicine makes him nervous, and he imagines that bad things are happening. Great-grandma is glad to have Twyla around because things are calmer when Twyla is there. The understanding, care, and love that Twyla gives to her great-grandpa allows her great-grandma to get some much-needed rest.

Twyla also loves her church. Every Sunday, she goes to services at the Good Shepherd Baptist Church, where she also sings in the children's choir. She's even there on Saturday to vacuum and dust!

At Columbine Elementary, Twyla is in the fifth grade in a program called "The Challenge Team." This class is made up of above-average third, fourth, and fifth graders. Twyla has been part of the

program since third grade. In addition to her academic work, Twyla is a leader on the student council, a member of the school news team, and a conflict manager on the playground.

As sergeant at arms for the student council, Twyla's job is to keep order during the meeting and call on members for ideas. She also works closely with Joe, the student-council president. Twyla and Joe have been best friends for two years, and they make a great team. Since Joe's cerebral palsy makes talking difficult for him, she listens carefully and makes sure that others understand him. It's a tough responsibility maintaining order at the meetings, keeping track of all the sales orders, and making sure that her friend Joe is understood. Twyla's patience, concern for others, and attention to detail help her succeed.

Every other Friday, the news team from her class covers the world news, national news, local news, weather, entertainment, special stories, editorials, and sports. They even make up their own commercials. Once, Twyla and Joe made up a commercial about charcoal cookies. Everyone laughed like crazy!

Twyla volunteers for a variety of reporting jobs, but her hand always shoots high into the air when the teacher asks for an entertainment reporter. She loves to share information about movies and music groups. Sometimes she even sings one of the songs in the top ten.

On Wednesdays during lunch recess, Twyla wears her purple t-shirt with the "Columbine School Conflict Manager" logo on the front. She uses her training and good sportsmanship skills to help students solve their problems. Her sense of humor comes in handy during some of the more challenging situations.

Twyla is like the Energizer bunny— she keeps going and going. Even as a fifth grader, she is a leader who makes other people feel special. She is a kid who really cares.

ROOSEVELT JOHNSON

The community in Selma, Alabama, changed for the better on September 3, 1972. That's the day Roosevelt Johnson was born, and after 22 years, he is still making things change in a positive way. How is Roosevelt making a difference? He believes that volunteering is the key to making the community a better place to live. In addition to volunteering 20 hours a week in community service, he is also codirector of the Black Belt Arts and Cultural Center (B-BACC).

Roosevelt was 12 years old when he became interested in volunteering. That's when his best friend introduced him to the B-BACC. Ms. Sanders and the other people at the center made a big difference in Roosevelt's life, so he decided to make a difference, too. Now its codirector, he encourages others to be involved at the center, and he has the privilege of working closely with his hero, Ms. Sanders.

B-BACC is a community center that

helps people deal with things that affect their lives, like education, teen pregnancy, gangs, and violence. It even has a tutoring service to help students with their school work. Sometimes there are special lessons that teach kids how to take the tests they need to get into college.

The center also sponsors a "Hang Out" week. It encourages kids to come in and spend time with their friends, giving them an opportunity to talk and listen to one another. It's a place where kids can hear African music, listen to a storyteller, or watch a play. Roosevelt acts in the plays that tell about real life problems in the community, such as teen pregnancy, abortion, drug abuse, or AIDS. Sometimes the problems are discussed in a group or rap circle. They hope that with everyone's input, solutions can be found.

Roosevelt's volunteer work isn't just at the B-BACC. He also helps elderly people clean up their houses, both inside and out. He uses newspaper and radio spots to let others know about the problems of bad housing. The elderly know that Roosevelt Johnson is a friend and a helper who really cares about them.

When the holidays roll around, Roosevelt finds himself asking local store owners to donate toys for needy children. He also raises money for a place that serves hot meals to those in need. Roosevelt not only helps in his community, he also reaches out to the world by helping raise money for Africare.

Roosevelt appreciates his mother's "old-fashioned" values. He is glad that she has taught him the difference between right and wrong. As a single parent, she worked hard to raise Roosevelt and his younger brother, Richard. Roosevelt has always been active in church, even though he remembers complaining about it when he was young. He is glad his mother helped him have a good relationship with Christ. His mother also taught him to keep his head up high and be proud of himself. Today, he is sharing these values with his family.

Every day is a challenge for Roosevelt Johnson, but he gives of himself to help people in need succeed against incredible odds. He feels strongly that everyone should get involved in some kind of community work. Roosevelt thinks that it's important to take time out to thank God for every new day and for your family.

JESSICA GRAY

"Do your best and get involved. Stay in school and out of trouble. Getting into trouble isn't worth it." That's 16-year-old Jessica Gray's advice to young people across the country. Her parents spend lots of time with her and teach her about life. They have taught her to stand up for what is right, get involved in community activities, and have fun helping others.

Jessica Gray is the only child of Jake and Janice Gray. Her father works for an insurance company. Her mother is an accountant. Both of her parents continue to have an active role in her busy life. Jessica and her mom are members of several community and church organizations. This gives them a chance to participate in social events and service projects together. Her dad takes Jessica to school, dance classes, and other meetings. He taught Jessica to drive and even fixed her hair when she was little.

Jessica feels she can ask her dad for advice about absolutely anything.

Jessica and her mother became members of the Jack and Jill organization when Jessica was 2½ years old. This group was started to get African American mothers and their children together once a month for cultural activities. The children keep scrapbooks and go to conferences every year. As the children get older, they do service projects for their community. Jessica has worked with other Jack and Jill members to collect clothing, food, and other things for Colorado Shares. Jessica likes helping others and making new friends.

Jessica Gray

The St. Peter Claver Society is another group that keeps Jessica and her mom involved in volunteer work. Janice Gray is in the Ladies' Auxiliary, and Jessica is in the Junior Daughters. St. Peter Claver was a Spaniard who nursed and fed the slaves on the slave cargo ships. He has been adopted as the African American's patron saint. The themes of this organization are Christian charity, friendship, and unity.

Volunteer work has given Jessica many wonderful new friends and special memories. One summer, boys and girls from Sacred Heart Catholic Church came to stay with children from Jessica's church. Together, they mowed lawns, built a wheelchair ramp, painted houses, and cooked at a soup kitchen for the homeless. Jessica also remembers bringing Easter baskets to a nursing home and reciting a poem she had written. Another time, she made valentines and cookies and collected magazines for senior citizens. Once, her youth group cooked a meal and served it to the older members of the church. Jessica enjoyed this because the young and old shared their stories, learning from one another.

Jessica is on the student council of her high school and plans to run again next year. She enjoys all of her classes and does well in them. Believe it or not, she even finds time to work at Taco Bell. Her goal is to become a genetic engineer, so she can work in a laboratory to study the way organisms are created.

Jessica Gray is an active, determined African American teenager who believes in God and knows where she is going in life. She is a caring person who daily demonstrates the Golden Rule— "Do unto others as you would have them do unto you."

DAMON K. JONES-SINGLETON

"Crack has got to die," Damon K. Jones-Singleton sings out to his audience. He is trying to comfort the victims of violent young criminals throughout the country. Twenty-one-year-old Damon has been in the same position as the criminals he sings about. But he turned his life around, and now he is helping others do the same. As an assistant director at Street Beat, Damon gives support to teens and tries to help them make positive changes in their lives.

His mother and father encouraged him to work hard in school and to be a success in his life. At school, Damon was a smart student who had lots of energy. He worked well with his teachers and really liked math and science. But when he was only 14 years old, Damon's life

Damon K. Jones-Singleton

changed dramatically. His father died suddenly, and Damon felt all alone. After school, he started getting in trouble with drugs, alcohol, and gangs.

In 11th grade, Damon was arrested. During his court appearance, the judge noticed that Damon's answers were intelligent and logical. Since he seemed smart and had once been successful in school, the judge decided to try to shock some sense into him. Damon had to spend three days in the Denver County jail. During this time, Dean Askew, the Executive Director of Street Beat, convinced Damon that he could make a difference in his life. All he had to do was try.

After the frightening few days in jail, Damon decided to get back on the right track. He decided he wouldn't hang around negative people or think negative thoughts. During his senior

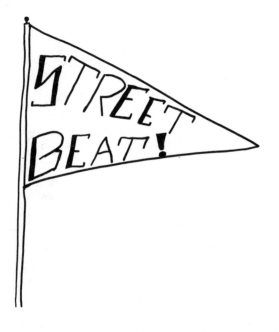

year in high school, Damon wrote the song "Young Men Die." That year, he also received an award as an outstanding young black man who turned his life around.

After high school, Damon went to Denver Community College. He also interviewed with and joined the group Up With People. This gave him the chance to travel throughout the United States and around the world. While traveling through Europe, Damon kept up with his college studies by taking correspondence courses.

Damon noticed that the architecture and culture changed from one country to the next, but that kids everywhere faced the same kinds of problems. He was able to share his story and encourage youth all over the world. This is the message that he shared with us. "You can change your life at any time. Pay attention! Read newspapers, watch the news, talk to people, look for ways to make a difference. Value what you have. Learn as much as you can. Don't take shortcuts. Take time to walk through life. When you run, you miss a lot."

When he returned to Colorado in July of 1994, Damon was offered the job of Assistant Executive Director at Street Beat. His goal is to graduate with a doctorate in child psychology, so he can continue to help young people change their lives.

In his songs, Damon uses a message of love and peace to help fight the battle against drugs. When someone asks him to sing, he wants them to listen to the words of "Young Men Die." Snapping his fingers to the beat, he begins to sing:

"Young men shot down twice
Brother seeks revenge and
Mothers cry, 'Oh when will it end?
Why do we have to die?'
Men are killing men
Causing gangs and wars in our lives.
Seems like love is gone and
Tears have filled our eyes.
Lord, help our lives and
Make it right."

DeSHONE TABB

DeShone was nervous about speaking in front of almost 600 freshman students at Rangeview High School, but she was running for class president and they were there to listen. From a strength within herself, DeShone found the courage to continue her speech.

"Don't vote for me because you know me," she said. "Vote for me because you know what I can do, and that I'll make a difference." She told the students that she was qualified and eager to represent them. She said she would set goals and do what it took to see that the goals were accomplished.

DeShone was born January 5, 1980. She lives with her grandparents, Janice and Douglas Alexander, and her younger brother. She is a member of Christ Our Redeemer Church and uses her leadership skills as president of the church's youth group. She often talks about grow-

DeShone Tabb

ing up and making wise choices. DeShone wants to set a good example for others, especially for her younger brother and cousin.

One Sunday, some kids were talking about a pregnant girl they thought was married. DeShone told them that the girl was only 13 and that she was not married. She shared information with them that she hoped might help them in the future. She told them that the best way to protect themselves from a teenage pregnancy is to practice abstinence. "If you are with someone who says, 'If you really love me, then let's have sex,'" said DeShone, "I would say, 'If you really love me, you'll wait until I'm ready.'" DeShone feels comfortable speaking her mind and telling people what is in her heart. She also encourages others to set personal goals.

One of DeShone's goals is to concentrate on her studies and bring her "B" average up to an "A". She is very interested in science and math. She would like to earn a degree in environmental law from Howard University.

Sports are another important part of DeShone's life. Her special love is basketball, and she wants to make the varsity basketball team as a sophomore. Her dad taught her the basic skills when she was six years old. She plans to go to a basketball camp during the summer to keep herself focused on her goal.

Helping others through community projects is another of DeShone's goals. At church, she participates in clothing and food drives for the needy. She once volunteered to pick up trash so that she could help make her community look better. DeShone enjoys finding something special in every new situation, and she has lots of fun volunteering.

DeShone Tabb has learned to stand up for what she believes, even if she stands alone. She encourages others to choose what is right, even if it's not popular. She is a true leader.

KEVIN PARKER

It was just another day in St. Paul, Minnesota. Kevin and his best friend, Jamal, were hanging out together. They had been best friends since they were little kids. They had just been to a basketball meeting at their high school. They were excited about the upcoming season, and both hoped to make the team's starting five. As soon as they got home, they did the usual—they made a big jug of grape Kool-Aid, cooked lots of chicken and rice, and sat down to watch the Michael Jordan videos they had already seen hundreds of times.

Later that night, they fell asleep. Jamal woke up the next morning when Kevin's grandmother came into the room. She was calling Kevin's name, but he didn't respond. Jamal laughed because he thought Kevin was playing one of his usual jokes. But Jamal and

Kevin's grandmother soon realized that Kevin wasn't joking. Jamal did everything he could to bring his best friend back to life, but nothing worked. Kevin had had a deadly asthma episode and died during the night. The way Jamal felt inside couldn't be explained.

Despite this tragic event, we want to share the good that came out of Kevin's life. It all began on April 20, 1977, when Kevin was born. He grew up with his mom, older sister, and grandma. As a child, Kevin was teased because of his allergies, which often caused a rash on his skin. Kevin had battled asthma since he was five. It was severe, and he always carried his inhaler.

Kevin loved basketball. He really admired Michael Jordan—he was always the first to buy Michael Jordan's newest shoes. Kevin had special permission

Kevin Parker

from his doctor to play basketball, and he took care of himself on the court, with his inhaler tucked safely in his sock. He played hard, inspiring other players on his team. Because Kevin was tall, he was "Mr. Shotblocker" for his team and their best rebounder. He had a great attitude. His sportsmanship rubbed off on the other players.

Besides playing basketball, Kevin also participated in the Inner City Youth League. This is a youth service organization that offers about 40 different activities for young people. It's more than a recreation center—kids can learn leadership and other skills that will help them in life. Kevin Parker became an important part of the Inner City Youth League. He started as their maintenance man, ordering all the supplies and keeping the keys to everything. The amount of trust that was handed over to this 17-year-old is proof of what a wonderful person Kevin was. He soon ran many things at the Youth League behind the scenes. He was a quiet hero.

Kevin was a big brother and a role model to many kids at Inner City. He helped run a summer program and often took 40 to 50 kids swimming or to the park. He used his leadership skills to work with Inner City Youth League's Intervention Corps. The Corps taught young people to solve their problems without violence. Students were trained to become mediators and to help other kids work through six steps to find a solution. He held this group together by taking his job seriously.

KEVIN
44
Parker

Kevin's funeral was held at St. Peter Claver, Kevin's church since childhood. It's difficult to explain the amount of love and respect that was crammed inside that church. Some people had to stand outside. Besides the smell of flowers, the smell of love was endless. The church walls were covered with posters on which people wrote their good-byes to him in their own special ways. His friends read many poems, letters, and stories. They told of how Kevin was there when people needed him most. He was like a big brother to some and a best friend to others. This love for Kevin continues today. People pray for Kevin every day and think of him constantly.

As you can see, Kevin was a hero to many people, even though he probably never knew it. After his death, people wanted to honor him. Kevin was named a "Future Hero" by KSTP television in Minneapolis for successfully tackling life despite difficult circumstances. They did a special news story that showed how Kevin touched others and how he was an everyday hero. The Inner City Youth League's Intervention Corps changed their name to the Kevin Parker Intervention Corps. The Mayor of St. Paul declared April 29, 1995, Kevin Parker Day. Kevin's mother even received a letter from Michael Jordan paying his respects. We know how much Kevin would have liked that!

You can be a hero like Kevin every day of your life. You can help your family cook, be a good friend, help other kids solve their problems, study hard in school, and work hard at sports. Remember, all heroes don't come with a big "S" on their shirt like Superman. They may just pass you in the hall every day, wearing Michael Jordan shoes.

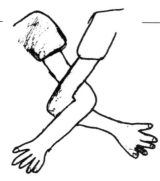

OUR VISION FOR A BETTER TOMORROW

There is a large problem in America today, one that has been around forever. We read about it in the newspaper, or friends tell us about it. It's on television, but we can even see it with our own eyes. Some people choose to ignore it, which is just another way of letting it continue. The problem is racism.

Racism is a whole way of looking at people. It involves a person thinking that he or she is better than another person because of religion, culture, or even something like their skin color. This way of thinking has led to discrimination against certain people. We have all run into someone who has made fun of us or people close to us, and it hurts. Actually, "racism" and "discrimination" are based on things that don't matter at all. We have to accept others for who they are. You don't have to be best friends with everyone, but you should give everyone a chance. This way, you might find things you have in common. The more you learn about another culture, the more you can learn about yourself.

We are trying to stop racism and discrimination now. We want all kids who read this book to stop judging others by their differences. We hope you will try to learn about your own heritage and share it with others in a way that shows you're open to hearing about their culture, too. What we're asking for is a lot, but if you take the time to get to know people as they really are, you will see how similar we all are.

WESTRIDGE YOUNG WRITERS WORKSHOP PARTICIPANTS

STUDENT AUTHORS

Aja Armstrong
Andra Arnold
Adrianna Baker
Katie Baker
Lizabeth T. Barnish
Jesse E. Julio Beason
LaRoy Bias
Nicole D. Bias
Adrian H. Bing
Shannon Boutwell
Bryan Brammer
Mara Jones-Branch
Kimberly L. Burnell
Ashley R. Carlson
Kirsten J. O. Carson
Benjamin C. Dallet
Jeremy N. Dillman
Brandon Dudley
Lindsey Dudley
Jacee Louise Elbeck
Jessie Ellis
Sarita Evans
Carrie Fann
Nancee Feagans
Josh Funderburg
James Fuqua
Laura Ann Fuqua
Matthew James Gallegos
Meleaha Glapion
Thomas Glapion
Michelle Renée Greene
Brooke Gustafson
Zach Haberler
Brittlee Hanson

Simone M. Hicks
Elisha L. Hill
Chinwuba Ikwuakor Jr.
Uzi C.B.N. Ikwuakor
Derek James
Jaquay Jenkins
Branden A. Johnson
Adrienne Jones
Andrea C. Kelly
Monticue A.C. Kimble
Jasmine M. Langford
Maurice L. Langford
Mechelle Love
Anthony B. Martin Jr.
James E. Martin
Janell M. Martin
Starr Martin
Aaron Martinez
Alisha L. Martinez
Jacob Edras Montoya
Karree Moore
Harrison D. Nealey
Brian J. Noble
Eric T. Noble
Mark Parker
Josh J. Pettit
Karlyda R. Poindexter
Amy Marie Pomranka
David M. Poppleton
Joseph Poppleton
Brian P. Quinn
Mary Elizabeth Robinson
Cliff M. Rodriguez
Paul Ruzzo

Teacher participants

TEACHER PARTICIPANTS

Shaz Sedighzadeh
Christopher Smith
Megan Stenbeck
Asheber P. Swanson
Sarah-Gayle Swanson
Bernicia Thompson
Courtney Ward
Brittni West-Ware
Aisha Williams
Chad Williams
Joloni Shane Williams
Naima N. Williams
Lindsay Ann Windels
Anthony Max Wright
Cecil J. A. Wright
Jamilah Wright
Carly L. York
Charles Youssef

Carneice Brown White, Consultant
Jean Tiran Cable, Assistant Director
Linda L. Carlson
Susan Chichester
Parke Covarrubias
Judith H. Cozzens, Director
Tom DeAngelo
Mary Ann Garcia-Pettit
Edith Glapion
Lorraine Gutierrez
Brenda F. Hale
Kathy Hayes
Helen Cozzens Healy
Jenny Hollanitsch
Adam Johnson
Betty Johnson

Mentors who assisted in the project

Stephanie Johnson
Zennetta Jones
Ivory Moore
Myrna Davis Nealey
Lorena E. Poppleton
Amy Sarah Pound, Assistant Director
Bettye J. Reed
Kent Rucker
Pearl J. Smith
Harold Thurman
Barb Weisz
Shireen I. Whitson
Lauren Wilhoite-Willis
Marianne E. Wright
Elaine Yarcho

MENTORS

These high school students assisted the younger students in writing the book:

Genesia E. Andrews
Shumara D. Andrews
Aspen Aletha Burkett
Channon Caston
Joshua J. Herald
Melissa Hicks
Rebecca K. Hill
Claire A. Imatani
Duane L. James
Michael Johnson
Dorothy Poppleton
Teisha Sheree Rollins
Nyeema A. Swanson
Akilah M. Thompson
Terrance Wright
Terrianne Wright

OTHER PARTICIPANTS

Craig Bowman, Consultant and Presenter
Bataki Camberlin, Presenter
Andrew Cozzens, Editor
Jack Cozzens, Business Manager
Marilyn Dallet, Volunteer
Billie Arlene Grant, Journalist
Kandance James, Consultant
Wallace Yvonne McNair, Consultant and
    Presenter
Abayomi Meeks, Presenter
Marci Moore, Presenter
Movement Free Dance Co., Presenters
Bill Potts, Presenter
Rose Roy, Organizational Assistant
Shelby Shrigley, Editor
Erle Swanson, Volunteer
Sergei Thomas, Presenter
Christopher S. Tucker, Photographer

Additions to this second edition of *Kids Explore America's African American*

Heritage were made by students at Columbine and St. Bernard Elementary schools.

Columbine Elementary

Sierra Armstrong
Julienne Bemski
Lauren Black
Jason Carey
Mark C. Fimberg
Joe Ford
Jerry J. Garcia
Emma G. Grant
Heidi M. Homburger
Tenishia Jones
Billy McCarren
Edward Mutegi
Rozelia Nelson
Genevieve Nuebel
Sydney H. Park
Ian Addison Philipp
David W. Rector
James G. Rector
Twyla Rivers
Sahada Sesay
Aysha K. Shehim
Veronica Wylie

Teachers:
Mae Davies
Susan Holmes
Shirley Merdes

St. Bernard's School

Jacob Anderson
Jennifer Anderson
Laura Anderson
Allison Bauer
Danielle Berndt

Joshua Blackburn
Becky Carr
Becky Chase
Amy Dorner
Adam Gibson
Jenny Hollanitsch
Adam Johnson
Stephanie Johnson
Florence Kimmel
Matt Krizanac
Frank Martin
Jake Mickus
Danielle Mondry
Julie Moore
Dan O'Brien
Jordan Pettis
Jesse Poolaw
Brian Raykowski
Jacob Robetor
David Rotter
Jessica Sachi
Chris Thomas
Marie VanCura
Mark Vaorderbruggen
Cory Weiss
Becky Wichlacz

Teachers:
Helen C. Healy
Barbara Weisz

CALENDAR

African Americans celebrate most of the holidays other Americans do, but they also celebrate holidays and festivals that are part of their culture. This calendar is a list of some important dates for African Americans. Occasions such as Martin Luther King Day and Black History Month take place across the U.S. Call to confirm dates and times.

January

African American Arts Festival, mid-January through mid-March, (North Carolina)—Celebrates cultural accomplishments of black artists. Includes visual and performing arts. For exact dates and locations, contact the United Arts Council of Greensboro, P.O. Box 877, Greensboro, NC 27402; (910) 333-7440.

Dr. Martin Luther King, Jr. Day Celebration, January 15, (Illinois)—Celebration includes a performance by a children's choir. Contact the Chicago Children's Museum, 700 East Grand Avenue, Chicago, IL 60611; (312) 527-1000.

February

Black History Month—Many museums, schools, and African American organizations across the U.S. sponsor events and celebrations that focus on African American heritage. Check your local newspaper during this month for any special events taking place near you.

African American History and Heritage Program, February 22–23, (Texas)—Two-day, family oriented cultural festival with vendors and exhibitors. Held annually during Black History Month. For date and location contact Dallas County Heritage Society, Old City Park, 1717 Gano St., Dallas, TX 75215; (214) 421-5141.

Artists' Salute to Black History Month, February 6–9, (California)—Exhibition of fine art by numerous artists of African

descent. Held annually during the first full week of February at the Plaza Pasadena. For more information contact Artists' Salute Coordinator, P.O. Box 36B75, Los Angeles, CA 90036-1203; (213) 939-0250.

June

Miami/Bahamas Goombay Festival, June 8–9, (Florida)—Festival commemorating the black heritage of Bahamians who settled in Miami during the 1800's. Vendors and special events. Held annually during the first full weekend in June. For further information contact Goombay Festival, 555 NE 15th St. #25K, Miami, FL 33132; (305) 372-9966.

Juneteenth, June 19, (Texas and other states)—Celebration commemorating the day in 1865 when Union General Granger conveyed the national order emancipating the slaves of East Texas.

　—Juneteenth Festival, June 14, (Washington, D.C.) Anacostia Museum at the Smithsonian Istitution, 1901 Fort Place SE, Washington, D.C. 20020; (202) 287-3382.

July

Summer Spectacular, July 8–14, (Indiana)—Large celebration held in Indianapolis including a wide variety of events for kids. For further information contact Indiana Black Expo, 3145 North Meridian, Indianapolis, Indiana 46208; (317) 925-2702.

August

African Marketplace and Cultural Fair, weekends, August 17–Labor Day, (California)—This fair presents food, art and music from numerous African cultures. Held annually during the months of August and September at Rancho Cienega Park. Contact the William Grant Still Art Center, 2520 Southwest View Street, Los Angeles, CA 90016; (213) 734-1164.

African-American Cultural Festival, August 15–16, (Tennessee)—Held at Miller's Plaza in Chattanooga, this event features performing artists and an African marketplace. Contact the Chattanooga African American Museum, 200 E. Martin Luther King Blvd., Chattanooga, TN 37403; (423) 267-1076.

African World Festival, August 16–18, (Michigan)—Celebration of African culture with art, food and music. Held at Hart Plaza, Detroit by the Museum of African American History, 301 Frederick Douglass, Detroit, MI 48226; (313) 833-9800.

September

African American Heritage Festival, September 14, (Maryland)—This event, held annually on the second Sunday in September, commemorates the contributions made by African Americans to the development of Worcester County, Maryland. For details, contact African American Heritage Committee, 10214 Old Ocean City Blvd., Berlin, MD 21811; (410) 641-3255.

Black Heritage Festival, September 14, (New Jersey)—Held annually in mid-July. Dancing, fine art, gospel and jazz music. For more information, contact the Black Heritage Festival, New Jersey Highway Authority, Garden State Parkway, Woodbridge, New Jersey 07095; (908) 442-8600.

Jubilee, September 7, (South Carolina)— Festival of black heritage with hands-on educational exhibits and entertainment. Contact Mann-Simons Cottage, 1403 Richland St., Columbia, SC 29201; (803) 252-1770.

Reston Black Arts Festival, (Virginia)— Held annually on Labor Day weekend at the Hunter Woods Village Center Atrium. Showcase of black art and culture in the Reston community. Contact, Reston Black Focus, P.O. Box 793, Reston, Virginia 22091; (703) 264-0468.

December

Junkanoo, December 26 (Nationwide)— Started long ago by Bahamian slaves, this event combines Mardi-Gras, African rituals and other traditions into a holiday with a strong emphasis on music, celebrated in various locations.

Kwanzaa, December 26–January 1 (Nationwide)—African American celebration in the spirit of traditional African harvest festivals. Combines elements of Thanksgiving,

Hanukkah and Christmas while stressing black unity, family and culture.

Miami Kwanzaa Festival, December 26–January 1 (Florida)—For more information, call the Miami Convention and Visitor's Bureau, 701 Brickell Avenue, Miami FL 33131; (800) 283-2707.

Detroit Kwanzaa Festival, December 26–January 1 (Michigan)—Sponsored by the Museum of African American History, 301 Frederick Douglass, Detroit, MI 48202; (313) 833-9800.

RESOURCE GUIDE

Here is a partial list of African American-related organizations that might be useful to you. There are more than 180 African American museums in the U.S. and many more cultural centers, publications, and associations that support African American culture. Dates, times, and admission prices change often, so please call ahead before you attend any event.

California

The Museum of African American Art, 4005 Crenshaw Boulevard, Third Level, Los Angeles, CA 90008; (213) 294-7071. This museum is devoted to interpreting, promoting, and preserving African American art. Open Wednesday to Saturday, 11 a.m.–6 p.m.; Sunday, 12 p.m.–5 p.m. Admission is free to everyone.

Afro-American Museum of History and Culture, Exposition Park, Los Angeles, CA 90037; (213) 744-7432. Open Tuesday through Sunday, 10 a.m.–5 p.m. Admission is free.

African American Historical and Cultural Museum, Fort Mason Center Bldg. C, Room 165, San Francisco, CA 94123; (415) 441-0640. Permanent and temporary

exhibits portraying the African American experience. The museum sponsors youth programs and African American history classes. Open Tuesday to Saturday, 11 a.m.–5 p.m. Admission is $2 for children; $3 for adults.

Colorado

Black American West Museum, 3091 California Street, Denver, CO 80205; (303) 292-2566. Features the many black cowboys of the American frontier. Open Wednesday to Friday, 10 a.m.–3 p.m.; Saturday, 10 a.m.–3 p.m.; Sunday, 2 p.m.–5 p.m. Admission is 50 cents for kids age 12 and under; $3 for adults.

Moyo Nguva Cultural Arts Center, 1648 Gaylord Street, Denver, CO 80206; (303) 377-2511. Dedicated to bringing quality art programs to low-income communities. Open Monday to Friday, 11 a.m.–6 p.m.; Saturday, 11 a.m.–2 p.m. Admission is free.

District of Columbia

National Museum of African Art, Smithsonian Institution, 950 Independence Avenue SW, Washington, D.C. 20560; (202) 357-4600. Extensive collection of art, books, and photographs portraying the African American experience. Open daily, 10 a.m.–5:30 p.m. Admission is free.

Florida

Museum of African American Art, 1308 N. Marion Street, Tampa, FL 33602; (813) 272-2466.

Georgia

The Tubman African American Museum, 340 Walnut Street, Macon, GA 31202; (912) 743-8544. The museum includes several exhibits, including a collection of

African and African American art and a showcase of inventions by black Americans. A week-long Heritage Camp for kids is held annually during the summer, with dance and music classes for kids throughout the school year. Open Monday to Saturday, 10 a.m. to 5 p.m.; Sunday, 2 p.m.–5 p.m. Admission is $1 for kids; $2 for adults.

Illinois

DuSable Museum of African-American History, 740 E. 56th Place, Chicago, IL; (312) 947-0600. One of the largest museums of its kind in the Midwest, the DuSable is dedicated to the history of Americans of African descent. Many kids' programs are offered throughout the year. Call ahead. Open Monday to Saturday, 10 a.m.–5 p.m.; Sunday, 12 p.m.–5 p.m. Admission is $1 for kids ages 6–12; $3 for adults. No charge for admission on Thursday.

Maryland

The Great Blacks in Wax Museum, 1601 E.

North Avenue, Baltimore, MD 21213; (410) 563-3404. More than 100 wax figures depicting famous African Americans. Also, African artifacts and African American history. Open Tuesday through Saturday, 9 a.m.–6 p.m.; Sunday, 12 p.m–6 p.m. Closed Monday except during summer. Admission is $3 for kids under age 12; $5.50 for adults.

Massachusetts

Museum of Afro-American History, Abiel Smith School, 46 Joy Street, Boston, MA 02114; (617) 742-1854. The museum's collections include historical artifacts, paintings, photographs, literary documents, and films. Holds special programs in Black History Month and summer, and throughout the year. Open daily from 10 a.m. to 5 p.m.

African Meeting House, 46 Joy Street 02114-4025; (617) 742-5415. Known as the oldest black church in the United States. Open Monday to Friday, 10 p.m.–4 p.m. Ranger-led tours during the summer leave from the Robert Gould Shaw Memorial directly across from the Statehouse at 10 a.m., 12 p.m., and 2 p.m. No charge for tours or admission to the Meeting House.

Museum of the National Center for Afro American Artists, 300 Walnut Avenue, Boston, MA 02119; (617) 442-8614. Exhibitions are wide-ranging, covering photography, painting, sculpture, and graphics from African, Carribbean, and African American artists. Open Tuesday to Sunday, 1 p.m.–5 p.m. Admission is $3 for students; $4 for adults; free for kids under age 12.

Michigan

Children's Museum, 67 E. Kirby Avenue, Detroit, MI 48202; (313) 494-1210. Standing exhibits include "Images of Southern Africa" and "Influence of African Tribes on African-Americans." Special exhibits offered during Black History Month.

Museum of African-American History, 301 Frederick Douglass, Detroit, MI 48202; (313) 833-9800. Features exhibits on the Underground Railroad in Michigan, African American art and African artifacts. Sponsors numerous special events during the year.

New Jersey

Afro-American Historical Society Museum, 1841 Kennedy Boulevard, Jersey City, NJ 07305; (201) 547-5262. Museum of black history since 1800, offering storytelling and art programs for children. Exhibits change monthly. Every December, the museum

sponsors a Kwanzaa program. Open Monday to Saturday, 10 a.m.–5 p.m. Before visiting the museum, call ahead to check on special events and activities.

New York

The Museum for African Art, 593 Broadway, New York, NY 10012; (212) 966-1313. Exhibits of African art as well as drumming, bead and gourd decorating workshops for kids. Open Tuesday to Friday, 10:30 a.m.–5:30 p.m.; Saturday and Sunday, 12 p.m.–6 p.m. Admission is $2 for children; $4 for adults.

African American Cultural Center, 350 Masten Avenue, Buffalo, NY 14209; (716) 884-2013. Hosts various historical and cultural activities with an emphasis on dramatic arts. Also holds summer day camp for children. Contact the center for a schedule of events and upcoming activities.

The Schomburg Center for Research in Black Culture, 515 Malcolm X Boulevard, New York, NY 10037; (212) 491-2200. Sponsors public programs for all members of the community. The Schomburg Center is considered one of the largest libraries of its kind in the U.S.

The Studio Museum in Harlem, 144 W. 125th Street, New York, NY; (212) 864-4500. Features one of the largest collections of art by Africans and African Americans. Programs for children include a cooperative program with schools. Open Wednesday to Friday, 10 a.m.–5 p.m; Saturday and Sunday, 1 p.m.–6 p.m. Admission is $1 for kids under age 12; $3 for students; $5 for adults.

North Carolina

Afro-American Cultural Center, 401 N. Myers Street, Charlotte, NC 28202; (704) 374-1565. Highlights include a standing exhibit of West African artifacts. Family art series first Saturday of each month. Call the center for information on upcoming events.

Mattye Reed African Heritage Center, NCAT State University, Greensboro, NC 27411; (910) 334-7874. The collection includes art and artifacts from more than 30 African countries. The center also offers education programs for children. Please call for more information.

Ohio

National Afro-American Museum and Cultural Center, 1350 Brush Row Rd., Wilberforce, OH 45384; (513) 376-4944. Various exhibits depicting aspects of black life in the U.S. Please contact the center for event information. Open Tuesday to Saturday, 9 a.m.–5 p.m.; Sunday, 1 p.m.–5 p.m. Admission is $1.50 for kids ages 5–18; $3.50 for adults.

Pennsylvania

Afro-American Historical and Cultural Museum, 701 Arch Street, Philadelphia, PA 19106-1557; (215) 574-0380. Collections include African artifacts, works by black artists and inventors and artifacts relating to the slave trade. Workshops for children dealing with exhibit themes.

South Carolina

Mann-Simons Cottage, 1403 Richland Street, Columbia, SC 29201; (803) 252-1770. Museum features many aspects of black life. It is housed in a cottage dating back to the 1850s.

Tennessee

Chattanooga African American Museum, 200 E. Martin Luther King Boulevard, Chattanooga, TN 37403; (423) 267-1076. Features Chattanooga's black history from 1850 to 1950, and reconstruction of an African hut. Open Monday to Friday, 9:30 a.m.–5 p.m.; Saturday, 12 p.m.–4 p.m. Admission is $1.50 for kids ages 6–12; $5 for adults.

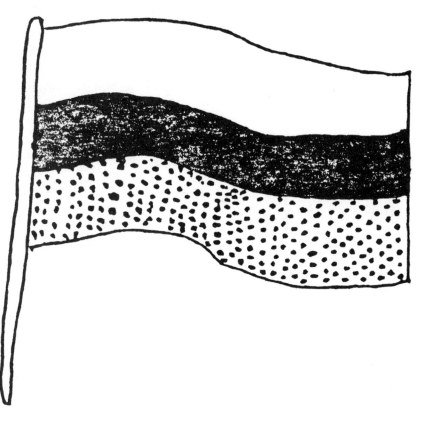

The National Civil Rights Museum, 450 Mulberry Street, Memphis, TN 38103; (901) 521-9699. Located at the assassination site of Martin Luther King Jr.. Remembers vital events of the Civil Rights Movement. Open Monday to Friday, 10 a.m.–5 p.m.; Sunday, 1 p.m.–5 p.m. Closed Tuesday. Admission is $3 for kids ages 6–12; $4 for students; $5 for adults.

Texas

African-American Museum, 3536 Grand Avenue, Dallas, TX 75210; (214) 565-9026. Exhibits include African American arts, crafts, and black history of Texas. Open Tuesday through Saturday, 12 p.m.–5 p.m.; Sunday, 10 a.m.–5 p.m. Admission is free.

Virginia

Black History Museum and Cultural Center, 00 Clay Street, Richmond, VA 23219;

(804) 780-9093. The museum has changing exhibits throughout the year, including those on African American contributions to painting, performing arts, photography, arts and crafts, civil rights movement, and more. Call ahead for special events. Open Tuesday to Saturday, 11 a.m.–4 p.m. Admission is $1 for children age 18 and under; $2 for adults. Closed on Monday.

Washington, D.C.

The Museum of African Art, 950 Independence Avenue, Washington, D.C.; (202) 357-1300. Celebrates African American contributions to painting, performing arts, photography, arts and crafts, civil rights movement, and more. Call ahead for special events and activities. Open seven days a week, 10 a.m.–5:30 p.m. Admission is free. Located at the Smithsonian Institution. Parking is limited; visitors are encouraged to use the subway.

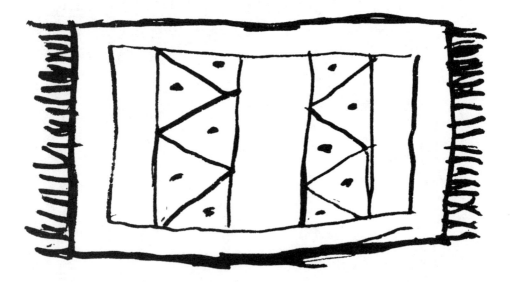

10003. This magazine, suited to junior high and high school students, features stories about African American youth and popular culture.

The Source: The magazine of hip-hop music, culture, and politics. Source Publications, 594 Broadway, Suite 510, New York, NY 10012. Intended for high school-age audience, this magazine covers a broad range of topics of interest to black youth.

YSB: The magazine for young sisters and brothers. Paige Publications, 1700 Moore Street, Suite 2200, Rosslyn, VA 22209. This publication is aimed at African American young adults. Covers a broad range of issues from music to financial planning.

Wisconsin

Black Holocaust Museum, 2233 North 4th Street, Milwaukee, WI 53212; (414) 264-2500. Displays relics, photos, and literature about the history of black oppression in America. Includes an hour-long video. Open from Monday to Saturday, 9 a.m.–6 p.m. Admission is $2.50 for kids ages 6–11; $5 for people age 12 and up.

Publications

Black Teen, Go-Stylish Publishing Company, 475 Par Avenue South, New York, NY 10016; (212) 689-2830. As the title suggests, this magazine covers a variety of subjects of interest to black teens.

Right On!, Sterling/McFadden Partnership, 233 Park Avenue South, New York, NY

INDEX

A

Abolitionists, 7
Adinkira art, 54-57
Affirmative Action, 25-26
Africa, geography, 2
Africa, history, 2-4
Ajulufoh, Georgette,
  105-106
Akhenaton, 3
Almanac, 31
American Federation of
  Labor, 11
Anacostia Museum, 75
Anderson, Marian, 47
Archives, 103-104
Art, 11, 53-57, 61-64
Artists, 43, 64, 110-111
Ashe, Arthur, 39-40

B

Bahamians, 75-76
Banneker, Benjamin, 31-32
Baseball, 32-33, 35-36
Bethune, Mary McLeod, 12,
  30, 81-82
Birmingham, Alabama,17
Biscuits, 81-82
Black American West
  Museum, 114
Black bottom dance, 71
Black cowboys, 32,
  113-115
Black, English, 98

Black history, father of, 46
Black History Month, 74, 77
Black Muslims, 18-20
Black Panthers, 20-21
Black Power Movement,
  18, 20
Blues, 45-46, 67
Blues, father of, 45-46
Braun, Carol Moseley, 27
Bread pudding, 86-87
Break dancing, 71
"Brer Rabbit Gets Brer
  Fox's Dinner," 91
Brooks, Gwendolyn, 48-49
*Brown v. Board of
  Education of Topeka,
  Kansas*, 13-14,
Bunche, Ralph 47-48

C

Cake, Emancipation Procla-
  mation Snackin', 88-89
Cakewalk, 69, 71
Calendar, 135-138
Camel walk, 71
Capoeira, 69
Carver, George Washing-
  ton, 30, 85
Catfish, 87-88
Celebrations, 74-79
Checker, Chubby, 71
Chisholm, Shirley, 27,
  37-38

Civil rights, 1, 10, 13,
  14-21, 24, 29, 34, 45
Civil War, 1, 7-10
Cleveland Indians, 32-33
Clinton, Bill, 27
Cloth, printing, 57
Coleman, Bessie,
Cornbread, 83
Cornmeal, 82-83
Corn pone, 83
Cosby, Bill, 38-39
Cotton, 5
Cotton gin, 5
Cowboys, 32, 113-115
Coye, 71

D

Dallas, Texas, 78-79
Dance, 11, 67, 69-73
Dancers, 72-73
Davids, Tice, 6
Davis, Angela, 20-21
Depression, Great, 12, 63
District of Columbia, 75
Dorantez, Estevanico, 41
Dorsey, Dr. Thomas, 66
Douglass, Frederick, 7
Drums, 57-59
Du Bois, W. E. B., 10-11

E

Education, 21-26, 38
Eisenhower, Dwight, 23

Egypt, 2
Emancipation, 7-9, 74-75
Emmaline, 62
Engineer, 42
Equiano, Olaudah, 42
Explorer, 41

F
Famous firsts, 29
Fields, Dorothy Jenkins,
    103-104
Floyd, Steve, 116-117
Folk artist, 110-111
Folk dancing, 69, 71
"Follow the Drinking
    Gourd," 96-97
Foods, 79-89
Football, 102
Freedom celebrations,
    74-75
Freedom rider, 17
Freeman, Elizabeth, 41-42

G
General, four-star, 36-37
Geometry, 4
Ghana, 54
Gibson, Althea, 49
Gompers, Samuel, 11
Gospel music, 66
Graffiti, 64
Gray, Jessica, 122-123
Greeks, 1-2
Greens, 84-85
Guitarist, 109-110

H
Haley, Alex, 51, 114
Handy, William Christo-
    pher, 45-46
Harambee, 78-79
Harlem Renaissance, 11, 63

Hastie, William, 13, 51
Heroes, 29
Hill, Hezekiah, 7
Hippocrates, 4
Hospital, Freedman's, 44
House of Representatives,
    U.S., 37
"How the Sea Creatures
    Found Their New
    Home," 94-95
"How the Turtle Got Marks
    on Its Shell," 93-94
Hughes, Frank, 106-108

I
Ice cream, "soul," 88
"I Have a Dream," 18
Imhotep, 3-4
Indians (Native Americans),
    4, 30, 41, 104
Inventors, 42, 43, 44-45

J
Jackson, Fatimah Linda
    Collier, 115-116
Jackson, Jesse, 27
James, Daniel "Chappie,"
    36-37
Jazz, 66-67
Jemison, Mae, 40-41
Jerry Rescue Day, 75
Jim Crow laws, 14, 17
Johnson, Roosevelt,
    120-122
Jones, Rodney, 109-110
Jones-Singleton, Damon,
    123-125
Juneteenth, 75
Junkanoo, 75-76

K
Kennedy, John F., 17

Kennedy, Robert, 17
Kenya, Africa, 2
King, Martin Luther Jr., 10,
    14, 16-18, 27, 74, 77-78,
    102
King, Rodney, 26-27
Kirk, Sylvia, 108-109
Korean War, 36, 104
Ku Klux Klan (KKK), 10
"Kumbaya," 65
Kush, 2-3
Kwanzaa, 76-77

L
Language, 98-99
LaNier, Carlotta Walls,
    21-24
Lewis, Edmonia, 43
Lincoln, Abraham, 7, 8-9, 75
Literature, 99-100
Little Rock Nine, 21-24
Los Angeles, California,
    26-27

M
McCoy, Elijah, 42
Malcolm X, 18, 20, 74, 78
Mali, 3
Mandingo, 3
March on Washington,
    18-19
Marshall, Thurgood, 13, 23,
    33-34
Matzeliger, Jan E, 43
Miami, Florida,103-104
Military, 12-13, 36-37, 104
"Mr. Civil Rights," 34
Montgomery Bus Boycott,
    14, 16, 17
Moors, 3
Morehead, Scipio, 62
Muhammad, Elijah, 18

Murals, 63–64
Musa, Mansa, 3
Museums, 64, 77, 112–113, 114
Music, 11, 45–46, 57–61, 64–69
Musicians, 68–69, 109–110
Muslims, 115–116

N
NAACP, 10, 34
National Council of Negro Women, 12
National Guard troops, 17, 22, 23
National Urban League, 10–11
Native Americans, 4, 41, 104
Niagara Movement, 10
Nigeria, Africa, 42
Nixon, E. D., 14, 16

O
Omaha, Nebraska, 78
Opera singer, 47
Organization for Afro-American Unity, 18
Owens, Jesse, 34–35, 114

P
Paige, Leroy B. "Satchel," 32–33
Parker, Kevin, 126–128
Parks, Rosa, 14
Peanut recipes, 85–86
Peas, black-eyed, 83–84
"The People Could Fly," 95–96
Physicians, 44
Pickett, Bill, 32
Pilot, 46

Pins, Adinkira, 54–55
Plantations, 5–6
Poet, 30, 48–49
Potts, Bill, 110–111
Presidential candidate, 27, 38
Price, Daryl, 102
Prince, Lucy Terry, 30
Pyramids, 3–4

R
Ragtime music, 66
Randolph, A. Philip, 11, 12, 13
Rap music, 67–68
Rattles, 59–61
Reagan, Ronald, 27
Reconstruction, 9–10
Renaissance, Harlem, 11–63
Resource Guide, 139–145
Rillieux, Norbert, 42
Rivers, Twyla, 118–120
Robinson, Jackie, 35–36
Rock 'n' roll, 66, 68, 69, 71
Roosevelt, Franklin D., 12
Rudolph, Wilma, 49–50
Rustin, Bayard, 12

S
St. Patrick, 1
Scientists, 40–41, 44–45, 115–116
Sculptors, 42–43
Servants, indentured, 4
Sharecroppers, 9, 63, 108
Ships, slave, 4–5
Simmons, Peter, 62
Singers, 46–47
Slavery, 1, 4–10, 41–42, 45, 61–62, 63, 64–66, 68–69, 71, 74–76, 80–81, 90–91, 96–97, 98, 99

Smith, Bessie, 47
Smith, Leon, 104–105
Soul food, 79–85, 88
Spirituals, 64–66, 67
Stewart, Paul, 113–115
Stories, 90–98
Supreme Court, U.S., 14, 22, 23, 33, 34
Supreme Court, Vermont, 30
Surgeon, 44
Sweet potato pie, 87

T
Tabb, DeShone, 125–126
"The Talking Eggs," 97–98
Tap-dancing, 69, 71
Tea, sassafras, 81
Teacher, 46, 108–109, 111–113
Tennis, 38–39, 49
Thomas, Clarence, 27
Thutmoses III, Pharaoh, 2
Truman, Harry, 13
Truth, Sojourner, 7
Tubman, Harriet, 7, 75
Turner, Henry Charles, 45
Twist, Chubby Checker's, 71–72

U
Underground railroad, 1, 6–7, 43, 75
United Negro College Fund, 26
University, first, 3
University of Colorado, 102
University of Maryland, 33

V
Vassa, Gustavus, 42
Vietnam War, 36, 104, 111

W

Walker, Sarah B., 44–45
Wallace, George, 17
Washington, Booker T., 10–11
Webb, Wellington, 27
Wells, Ida B., 45
White, Carneice Brown, 111–113
Whitney, Eli, 5, 17
"Why Spiders Have No Hair," 95
Wilder, Douglas, 27
"Wiley and the Hairy Man," 91–93
Williams, Daniel Hale, 44
Woods, Granville T., 43–44
Woodson, Carter, 46
Works Progress Administration, 63
World War II, 12

American Origins Series

Each is 48 pages and $12.95 hardcover.
Tracing Our English Roots
Tracing Our German Roots
Tracing Our Irish Roots
Tracing Our Italian Roots
Tracing Our Japanese Roots
Tracing Our Jewish Roots
Tracing Our Polish Roots

Bizarre & Beautiful Series

Each is 48 pages, $14.95 hardcover, $9.95 paperback.
Bizarre & Beautiful Ears
Bizarre & Beautiful Eyes
Bizarre & Beautiful Feelers
Bizarre & Beautiful Noses
Bizarre & Beautiful Tongues

Extremely Weird Series

Each is 32 pages and $5.95 paperback.
Extremely Weird Bats
Extremely Weird Endangered Species
Extremely Weird Fishes
Extremely Weird Frogs
Extremely Weird Reptiles
Extremely Weird Spiders
Extremely Weird Birds
Extremely Weird Insects
Extremely Weird Mammals
Extremely Weird Micro Monsters
Extremely Weird Primates
Extremely Weird Sea Creatures
Extremely Weird Snakes

Kids Go!™ Travel Series

Each is 144 pages and $7.95 paperback.
Kids Go! Atlanta (avail. 1/97)
Kids Go! Cleveland (avail. 2/97)
Kids Go! Denver
Kids Go! Minneapolis/St. Paul

Kids Go! San Francisco
Kids Go! Seattle
Kids Go! Washington, D.C.
(avail. 1/97)

Kids Explore Series

Written by kids for kids, each is $9.95 paperback.
Kids Explore America's African American Heritage, 160 pages
Kids Explore America's Hispanic Heritage, 160 pages
Kids Explore America's Japanese American Heritage, 160 pages
Kids Explore America's Jewish Heritage, 160 pages
Kids Explore the Gifts of Children with Special Needs, 128 pages
Kids Explore the Heritage of Western Native Americans, 128 pages

Masters of Motion Series

Each is 48 pages and $6.95 paperback.
How to Drive an Indy Race Car
How to Fly a 747
How to Fly the Space Shuttle

Rainbow Warrior Artists Series

Each is 48 pages, $14.95 hardcover, $9.95 paperback.
Native Artists of Africa
Native Artists of Europe
Native Artists of North America

Rough and Ready Series

Each is 48 pages and $4.95 paperback.
Rough and Ready Homesteaders

Rough and Ready Cowboys
Rough and Ready Loggers
Rough and Ready Outlaws and Lawmen
Rough and Ready Prospectors
Rough and Ready Railroaders

X-ray Vision Series

Each is 48 pages and $6.95 paperback.
Looking Inside the Brain
Looking Inside Cartoon Animation
Looking Inside Caves and Caverns
Looking Inside Sports Aerodynamics
Looking Inside Sunken Treasure
Looking Inside Telescopes and the Night Sky

Other Children's Titles

Habitats: Where the Wild Things Live, 48 pages, $9.95

The Indian Way: Learning to Communicate with Mother Earth, 112 pages, $9.95

Ordering Information

Please check your local bookstore for our books, or call **1-800-888-7504** to order direct and to receive a complete catalog. A shipping charge will be added to your order total.

Send all inquiries to:
John Muir Publications
P.O. Box 613
Santa Fe, NM 87504